100

Best Foods for
Pregnancy

The healthiest foods for you and your baby including 100 delicious recipes

Charlotte Watts

First published in 2011
LOVE FOOD is an imprint of Parragon Books Ltd

Parragon
Queen Street House
4 Queen Street
Bath BA1 1HE, UK

ISBN: 978-1-4454-5369-9

Printed in Indonesia

Created and produced by Ivy Contract
New photography by Clive Streeter
Additional recipes by Nicola Graimes

Notes for the Reader
This book uses both metric and imperial measurements. Follow the same
units of measurement throughout; do not mix metric and imperial. All
spoon measurements are level: teaspoons are assumed to be 5 ml, and
tablespoons are assumed to be 15 ml. Unless otherwise stated, milk is
assumed to be full fat, eggs and individual vegetables are medium, and
pepper is freshly ground black pepper.

The times given are an approximate guide only. Preparation times differ
according to the techniques used by different people and the cooking
times may also vary from those given. Optional ingredients, variations
or serving suggestions have not been included in the calculations.

Pregnant and breastfeeding women are advised to avoid eating raw
meat, eggs, fish and shellfish, smoked or cured meats and fish, soft and
blue-veined cheeses, alcohol, caffeine, all pâtés and unpasteurized dairy
products. For further advice, read the information in the introduction on
foods to avoid. Sufferers from nut allergies should be aware that some of
the ready-made ingredients used in the recipes in this book may contain
nuts. Always check the packaging before use.

Nutritional data obtained from the USDA national nutrient database.

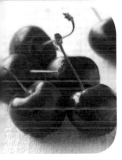

CONTENTS

INTRODUCTION

When you are pregnant, your body requires more vitamins, minerals and essential fatty acids right from the moment of conception. In this book we will guide you through the foods and diet that will best help you achieve the healthiest pregnancy for the wellbeing of both you and your baby.

Good nutrition can help you to remain fully active during pregnancy and keep up your energy levels so that you can look after your newborn and recover more quickly post-birth. This means preparing as much food as possible yourself from fresh, whole ingredients rather than relying on processed food. It is important to follow current government guidance on food, drink and activity for a healthy pregnancy. No single food has any special nutrients or powers that can change the overall health of individuals; it is the combination of food, drink and lifestyle, and making balanced choices, that can provide the nutrients and energy your body needs for a healthy pregnancy.

Weight before, during and after pregnancy

Addressing weight issues needs to happen before conception. This includes gaining weight if you are under your ideal weight to support production of the hormones you need to conceive. If you are overweight, talk to your doctor or healthcare provider about your ideal weight to help increase your fertility and lessen the risk of pregnancy complications such as diabetes and high blood pressure. Weight loss is not advised during pregnancy.

Normal weight gain during pregnancy is between 11.3 kg and 15.9 kg (25–35 lb), but will depend on your build and height. On average, this is 350–400 g (¾–⅞ lb) per week after the first trimester. Even though your heart rate and nutrient needs increase during pregnancy, you don't have to consume more calories until the third trimester, when your requirements go up by about 10 per cent. Morning sickness can cause weight loss, so building up your appetite to regain weight when it passes is crucial.

Until at least 6 weeks after birth, focus on eating healthily, rather than losing weight. Weight loss will occur naturally and safely without hindering your recovery if you concentrate on eating regular meals and avoiding convenience foods wherever possible.

General dietary guidelines

A mother's diet needs to supply all of the energy and nutritional needs of the developing foetus, as well as her own, so a consistent, healthy and varied diet is essential:

- Eat regular meals and never skip breakfast – you need regular energy and your baby needs a constant fuel supply for optimum growth and development. Breakfast keeps these levels sustained throughout the day, lessens cravings for unhealthy foods later and allows you to avoid 'highs and lows' of energy and mood.
- Snack healthily – especially if your appetite is lowered, or your growing bump means you eat less at meals because there is less room in your stomach. Even if you feel nauseous or lacking in appetite, try to eat something healthy at least every 4 hours. The occasional treat is fine.
- Aim to eat more in the lead up to the birth – you will need the energy stores both for labour and for recovery afterwards. This may need to be little and often as your bump allows for less easy digestion.
- Stay hydrated – from conception to breastfeeding, your body needs fluids to keep eliminating harmful toxins, supporting the immunity of mother and baby, and maintaining the growth of the foetus.

Specific nutritional considerations

Extra protein – your needs increase by up to a third during pregnancy because it is used to build your baby's body. Lean meat, certain fish (see pages 10–11 for more information), eggs (thoroughly cooked), pasteurized dairy produce and vegetable proteins (tofu, beans, nuts, seeds and pulses) are good sources. Protein should be included in every meal.

Healthy oils and fats are required constantly – fertility, pregnancy hormones, your recovery after birth and your baby's organs (like heart, liver and brain) rely on their daily intake. Oily fish such as salmon (wild or organic), mackerel, herring, sardines, fresh anchovies, trout and pilchards provide omega-3 fatty acids and are safe to consume while pregnant but do not eat them more than twice a week. Do not take cod liver oil supplements when pregnant – they contain very high levels of vitamin A, which may lead to birth defects. Vegetarian foods such as green leafy vegetables, and moderate amounts of nuts and seeds, provide omega-3 and omega-6 fatty acids. Healthy monounsaturated fats are found in avocados, walnuts and olive oil.

Complex carbohydrates – these are rich in fibre, B vitamins, folic acid (folate), iron and magnesium, which all support pregnancy. They are also particularly good for easing constipation, a common pregnancy problem. A diet rich in beans, pulses, wholegrains and vegetables will provide these constant energy sources.

Iron intake is important during pregnancy as your body makes extra red blood cells. Iron-rich proteins are particularly beneficial (meat, beans, eggs and tofu). Green leafy vegetables provide both iron and vitamin C, the latter needed for iron's absorption. Vegetarians and vegans will need to have their iron levels monitored by their doctor and may require a supplement.

Calcium intake must be kept up during pregnancy and if breastfeeding, to support the formation and growth of your baby's skeleton. As well as dairy produce, green leafy vegetables, nuts and seeds are good sources of this mineral. These also provide magnesium, which is also needed for bone development.

Fruit and vegetables are rich in immune-supporting antioxidants such as vitamins C, E and zinc. Different colours provide different benefits and so variety is essential. Consuming at least five portions a day – two servings of fruit and at least three of vegetables – may help to support a mother's immunity and provides a good supply of vitamin C, needed for healthy bones, skin and collagen production.

Using this book

Many of the foods in this book are healthy during every stage of pregnancy. However some are included for specific reasons at a particular stage and may have contraindications at another – for example, foods that promote breast milk flow are not advised during pregnancy. Read each entry and build up a varied and tasty diet from the foods available to you before including. Any herbs mentioned in this book should be eaten only in normal culinary use and avoided in larger

medicinal amounts. Discuss any changes in your diet with your doctor or healthcare provider. There is a comprehensive table of specific foods to avoid during pregnancy on pages 10–11.

Key to recipe codes
Recipes within the book are accompanied by the following codes:

(G) Growth of baby – contains nutrients that particularly support full and healthy growth of your baby's body.

(B) Brain development of baby – particularly supportive of constant growth of brain cells and future cognitive function of your baby.

(A) Immunity-supporting antioxidants – substances that help prevent infection, inflammation and tissue damage that can affect fertility, pregnancy and recovery.

(N) Natural remedy – has specific properties shown to help relieve common pregnancy and post-pregnancy symptoms, often with a long history of traditional use.

(V) Suitable for vegetarians.

(Q) Quick and easy to prepare.

Foods to avoid or reduce while pregnant

Certain foods must be avoided during pregnancy to reduce the risk of harm to mother and baby – for a full list, consult the chart overleaf. Official advice on what is safe to eat during pregnancy can change, so always consult your doctor or healthcare provider for the latest information.

There are a number of foods that are inherently deemed 'unhealthy' and offer high calories with little nutritional value, known as 'empty calories'. They are usually processed, refined and high in sugar, salt and unhealthy fats, often having been fried or the fats damaged in the cooking process. These present a risk in pregnancy not just because of their lack of supportive nutrients, but also because they may reduce the body's immune, circulatory and detoxification ability. They may also contribute to cell damage and increase your need for more protective antioxidant nutrients such as vitamin C and E. Note that convenience foods and ready-made meals tend to be high in salt, unhealthy fats and chemical additives, so are best avoided during pregnancy.

Refined foods such as sugar, white flour and white rice are termed 'simple carbohydrates' and provide little nutritional value or fibre. They are quickly digested, causing sudden rises in blood sugar that may lead to low energy and the loss of vital pregnancy nutrients. Those with high fat and refined sugars, e.g. pastries, cakes and biscuits, are the most unhealthy.

Hydrogenated vegetable oils found in margarines may interfere with the body's utilization of essential fatty acids. Check labels – foods containing hydrogenated fats are usually highly processed and may contain other undesirable chemical additives.

Burnt fats are known to be harmful to the body because they contain high levels of free radicals, which can damage cells and tissues. Avoid over-cooked meats and charred barbecue food.

Note that it is now considered safe to eat foods containing peanuts during pregnancy unless there is a family history of allergy or your healthcare provider advises you not to.

A word on colic, reflux and gas in breastfed babies

There is much discussion on which foods may or may not cause digestive issues in breastfed babies, and many cultures differ in opinion. Although evidence suggests that the factors which cause gas in the mother do not actually reach breast milk, individual mothers cite different foods that they observe affecting their babies. Consider foods that you may not tolerate as potential problems, and monitor your baby after you eat different foods. Bear in mind that colic, reflux and gas problems are an issue of the baby's underdeveloped digestion, and time is the best healer.

Specific pregnancy risk factors

Risk factor/risk	Foods/substances to avoid
Listeria infection Rare, but can cause flu-like illness linked to miscarriage, stillbirth or severe illness in newborn babies	• All types of pâté, even vegetarian • Soft and blue-veined cheeses, e.g. Stilton, Brie • Ready-made meals; insufficiently reheated food
Salmonella infection Food poisoning will not directly harm the baby but may make the mother very unwell	• Raw meat, poultry and fish • Unpasteurized milk • Raw eggs and raw egg products
Campylobacter infection Bacterial infection linked to miscarriage and premature labour	• As for salmonella – see above • Untreated water
Toxoplasmosis infection Rare, but infection can lead to serious problems for the baby	• Raw or undercooked meat • Cured meat such as salami and Parma ham • Soil; cat faeces
Dioxins and PCBs Harmful pollutants, such as dioxins, PCBs and methyl mercury, can be found in fish	• Limit to two portions of oily fish per week • Avoid shark, swordfish, tilefish, king mackerel – all particularly high in mercury
Xenoestrogen exposure Hormone disruptor that may interfere with pregnancy hormones	• Soft plastics; pesticides, herbicides and fertilizers; meat and dairy containing growth hormones
High concentrations of vitamin A High intake in pregnancy has been linked to a higher than average risk of birth defects	• Liver, or liver-containing products such as pâté • Cod liver oil • Multivitamin supplements containing vitamin A
Parasitic infection, e.g. tapeworm Digestive upsets that may lead to severe food poisoning	• Undercooked or raw shellfish
Caffeine A stimulant that in large amounts may deplete calcium and raise blood pressure; possible link to miscarriage in high doses	• Tea and coffee • Colas, energy drinks and chocolate • Some medications
Alcohol Intake has been linked to a reduction in birth weight, and also birth defects and miscarriage	• All wines, beers and spirits/liquors
Salt Added to food and in processed foods can contribute to high blood pressure	• Added table salt • Processed and convenience foods
Herbs Outside of normal culinary use, herbs in large doses can interfere with pregnancy hormones	• Large amounts of herbal teas • Herbal supplements

Alternatives/action

- Hummus and guacamole make good alternatives
- Eat hard cheeses like Cheddar
- Ensure food is cooked all the way through and reheated properly

- Check raw meat and fish is stored safely and cooked thoroughly; wash hands after preparing. Avoid sashimi
- Check labels, although most dairy is now pasteurized
- Only eat eggs cooked until white and yolk are solid; avoid homemade mayonnaise/mousse with raw eggs

- As for salmonella – see above
- Drink clean water and bottled water if sources are unsure

- Check meat is cooked thoroughly
- Choose uncured cold meats such as turkey or chicken slices
- Wash all fruit and vegetables; do not handle litter trays

- Oily fish include mackerel, sardines, salmon and trout. Canned tuna and/or tuna steaks are also advised two times a week maximum. Supplement if necessary with omega-3 fatty acid supplements designed for use during pregnancy – check with your healthcare provider

- Avoid storing fatty foods in soft plastics (e.g. clingfilm); avoid microwaving foods in plastic – transfer foods to glass containers or cook conventionally. Wash fruit and vegetables before eating. Consider buying organic meat, dairy and eggs where possible

- Choose alternative protein sources such as turkey or beef. Avoid all pâtés
- Omega-3 fatty acid supplements designed for use during pregnancy – check with your healthcare provider
- Prenatal supplements that contain vitamin A in the form of beta carotene are safe to consume

- Ensure all shellfish are cooked thoroughly

- Wean off tea and coffee to just one or two cups a day with food; avoid if possible
- Avoid colas and energy drinks, and limit chocolate to a treat
- Check with your healthcare provider

- Safe limits are inconclusive so best to avoid

- Celery salt or spices

- Vary herbal teas and limit to one or two cups a day (see our guidelines for entries in this book)
- Avoid all herbal supplements in pregnancy and while breastfeeding
- Check with a medical herbalist for herbs used for fertility

Fertility and Conception

In the preparation stage before pregnancy, the nutritional focus is on increasing the nutrients needed for egg and sperm health and reducing the factors that may harm these. Vitamins A and C and other antioxidants can help protect the egg and sperm from damage by chemicals and pollutants. Low levels of zinc may affect fertility in both men and women, while folic acid levels have to be high to help prevent birth defects. Good dietary protein levels are also required for conception.

In this chapter we focus on foods that provide dense nutritional content, and that offer an alternative to processed foods, caffeine and high-sugar foods that may affect fertility. Guidelines also support weight loss before pregnancy, the safe time for any excess to be lost.

(G) Growth of baby

(B) Brain development of baby

(A) Immunity-supporting antioxidants

(N) Natural remedy

(V) Suitable for vegetarians

(Q) Quick and easy to prepare

01

PUMPKIN SEEDS

Seeds, which encapsulate all that is necessary for the beginnings of plant life, contain high levels of the nutrients needed for fertility.

MAJOR NUTRIENTS PER 15 G/½ OZ PUMPKIN SEEDS

Kcalories	81
Total fat	6.9 g
Monounsaturated fat	2.44 g
Omega-6 fatty acids	3,105 mg
Omega-9 fatty acids	2,122 mg
Protein	4.53 g
Carbohydrate	1.61 g
Fibre	0.9 g
Vitamin B1	0.04 mg
Vitamin B3	0.75 mg
Vitamin B5	0.11 mg
Vitamin E	1.64 mg
Magnesium	88.8 mg
Potassium	121.4 mg
Phosphorus	184.95 mg
Iron	1.32 mg
Manganese	0.68 mg
Selenium	1.41 mcg
Zinc	1.17 mg

Pumpkin seeds contain particularly high levels of zinc, which is needed for all aspects of reproductive health, including healthy hormones and eggs, and creating new cells for growth. These precious seeds are also an excellent source of vitamin E, the most important antioxidant when it comes to protecting eggs from damage. The vitamin E works together with the selenium content to help create a healthy womb lining, ready for fertilization and implantation. Pumpkin seeds are also one of the best plant sources of omega-3 fatty acids, and deliver these in good balance with omega-6 fatty acids – in combination, these two play a vital role in keeping the oily outer layer of an egg intact.

- Contains zinc, which is essential for reproduction.
- Vitamin E content and high levels of essential fatty acids keep eggs healthy and primed for fertilization.
- Contain vitamin E and selenium in an effective combination to ensure the optimum womb environment for conception.

Practical tips:

Store pumpkin seeds in airtight jars away from heat and light in order to keep the easily perishable essential fatty acids and vitamin E from damage that can affect their potency. Eat these seeds as healthy snacks in place of sugary foods that may reduce fertility. Add to salads to provide extra protein and healthy fat content.

Couscous, chickpea and pumpkin seed pilaf

SERVES 4 Ⓖ Ⓐ Ⓥ Ⓠ

200 g/7 oz barley couscous
350 ml/12 fl oz vegetable stock
1 large yellow pepper, deseeded
    and chopped
4 spring onions, chopped
10 ready-to-eat dried apricots,
    chopped
50 g/1¾ oz sultanas
50 g/1¾ oz flaked almonds
50 g/1¾ oz walnut pieces
1 tbsp pumpkin seeds
150 g/5½ oz canned chickpeas,
    drained and rinsed
2 tbsp pumpkin seed oil

Method

1 Put the couscous in a large, heatproof bowl. Heat the stock in a saucepan to boiling point, then pour over the couscous and stir well. Cover and leave to stand for 15 minutes, by which time all the liquid should have been absorbed.

2 Stir all the remaining ingredients, except the oil, into the couscous, forking through lightly. Serve drizzled with the oil.

02 LEMONS

Lemon is an extremely useful and versatile ingredient. It will increase the cleansing and detoxifying actions of the body that are so important for conception.

Lemons are very high in vitamin C, a major antioxidant that helps protect eggs and the uterine wall – as well as sperm – from damage from toxins. Their cleansing effect is heightened by their alkalizing action inside the body. Although they taste very acidic, once eaten, lemons actually help to balance our acid:alkaline levels. This balance is crucial in women for their hormones to work efficiently and to ensure a hospitable environment for sperm. In men, it allows the body to store sperm safely. The high potassium level in lemons also ensures that fluid reaches the cells, keeping the body hydrated, and helps to maintain healthy mucous levels within the female reproductive organs, which enables egg implantation.

• Very high in vitamin C, which protects the egg and womb from pollutants that can interfere with fertilization.
• Keep the body in an alkaline state, so promoting optimum hormone function and hydration.
• Keep digestion efficient so that you get the most nutrients possible from your diet.

Practical tips:
Lemon juice is an excellent flavouring in dressings. Use in place of vinegars because these may exacerbate yeast and digestive problems. Lemon juice also tastes great with water, in place of a sugary cordial. For the most cleansing effect, make the water hot and add the juice of up to half a lemon.

DID YOU KNOW?

In traditional Chinese medicine, lemon water has been prescribed to boost fertility for centuries. It is believed to increase hydration while also flushing out toxins from the body.

MAJOR NUTRIENTS PER MEDIUM-SIZED LEMON

Kcalories	17
Total fat	0.17 g
Protein	0.64 g
Carbohydrate	5.41 g
Fibre	1.6 g
Vitamin C	30.7 mg
Potassium	80 mg

Chickpea, saffron and lemon chermoula soup

SERVES 4–6 (A) (N) (V)

2 tbsp olive oil

1 leek, sliced

1 onion, chopped

1 stick celery, sliced

1 carrot, sliced

2 cloves garlic, crushed

1 tbsp coriander seeds

115 g/4 oz canned tomatoes

140 g/5 oz canned chickpeas,
    drained and rinsed

1 litre/1¾ pints vegetable stock

1 potato, cubed

2 bay leaves

pinch of saffron strands

2 lemons, halved, cut sides charred
    for 2–5 minutes in a hot
    non-stick frying pan

Chermoula

2 cloves garlic, finely sliced

½ red chilli, finely chopped

1 tsp paprika

1 tsp ground cumin

1 tsp lemon juice

2 tsp white wine vinegar

4 tbsp finely chopped fresh
    flat-leaf parsley

4 tbsp finely chopped fresh
    coriander leaves

Method

1 Heat the oil in a large saucepan and sauté the leek, onion, celery,
   carrot and garlic, stirring constantly, for 5 minutes, or until softened
   but not coloured. Add the coriander seeds and cook for a further
   2 minutes.

2 Add the tomatoes, chickpeas, stock, potato, bay leaves and saffron.
   Stir well and bring to the boil. Reduce the heat, cover and simmer
   for 20 minutes, or until the vegetables are tender.

3 To make the chermoula, pound the garlic and chilli with the spices,
   lemon juice and vinegar to a smooth paste in a mortar with a pestle.
   Transfer to a saucepan, add the herbs and gently warm for
   5 minutes to infuse the flavours. Do not boil.

4 Remove the bay leaves, then blend the soup using a food processor
   or blender. Pass through a medium sieve into warmed soup bowls.
   Top with the chermoula and serve with the charred lemons for
   squeezing over.

03

FREE-RANGE EGGS

Each egg is a microcosm of potential fertility. They contain the best sources of protein available when it comes to supporting both egg and sperm health.

Eggs encapsulate the possibility of new life, and so contain all the valuable nutrients needed to support it. Their balanced and rich fat content enables the production of the hormones oestrogen and progesterone, needed for conception, and their record-breaking B-vitamin status helps a woman to use those hormones in the best way possible. High levels of selenium and sulphur also help to remove toxic metals, such as lead and mercury, which can interfere with fertility, while the vitamin A in eggs protects both sperm and egg from damage that can affect fertilization. Eggs contain both folate (folic acid) and choline, which have been shown to work together to prevent spina bifida and other neural tube defects in the foetus.

MAJOR NUTRIENTS PER MEDIUM-SIZED EGG

Kcalories	63
Total fat	4.37 g
Monounsaturated fat	1.68 g
Omega-6 fatty acids	505 mg
Omega-9 fatty acids	1,582 mg
Protein	5.53 g
Carbohydrate	0.34 g
Vitamin A	214 IU
Vitamin D	22 IU
Vitamin B2	0.21 mg
Vitamin B5	0.63 mg
Vitamin B12	0.57 mcg
Choline	110.5 mg
Iron	0.81 mg
Selenium	13.9 mcg
Zinc	0.49 mg
Lutein/Zeaxanthin	146 mcg

- Contain the right kind of fats, which act as building blocks in the body's production of fertility hormones.
- Sulphur and selenium remove toxic substances that can interfere with conception.
- Vitamin A and protein help keep eggs and sperm in optimum condition.
- Choline and folic acid content help prevent spina bifida.

Practical tips:
Buy organic free-range eggs where possible to avoid ingesting unwanted hormones that may interfere with conception and increase the risk of bacterial infection. Purchase from a reliable source. Having eggs for breakfast helps promote sustained energy levels.

Tomato frittata

SERVES 4 (G) (A) (V) (Q)

6 large eggs
2 tbsp chopped fresh basil
2 tbsp olive oil
1 small onion, sliced
2 large ripe tomatoes, halved,
    deseeded and thinly sliced
pepper
rocket leaves, tossed in balsamic
    vinegar and extra virgin olive oil,
    to serve

Method

1 Beat the eggs in a bowl then stir in the basil and season with
    pepper to taste; set aside.
2 Heat 1 tablespoon of the oil in a 25-cm/10-inch non-stick frying pan
    over a medium heat. Add the onion and fry for 5–7 minutes until
    softened, but not browned.
3 Add the tomatoes to the pan and fry for about 30 seconds, or until
    they start to soften. Carefully tip the onion and tomatoes into the
    bowl containing the eggs.
4 Wipe the frying pan with kitchen paper and reheat over a medium–
    high heat. Add the remaining oil and heat, swirling it around to coat
    the sides. Pour in the eggs and tomatoes and leave to cook for 5–6
    minutes, shaking the pan occasionally and working the set frittata
    into the centre so the uncooked egg runs underneath.
5 Gently slide the frittata out of the pan onto a large, flat plate. Place
    the pan upside-down over the frittata, then, using an oven glove,
    invert the pan and plate, so that the uncooked side is on the
    bottom. Continue to cook for a further 3–4 minutes until the frittata
    is fully cooked and set throughout.
6 Slide the frittata onto a plate and serve warm, or leave to cool and
    serve at room temperature. Cut into wedges and serve with the
    dressed rocket leaves.

04

BROCCOLI

One of the true superfoods, broccoli has fantastic detoxifying qualities that help prepare a woman's reproductive system for conception and a healthy pregnancy.

All of the cruciferous vegetables – broccoli, Brussels sprouts, cabbage, cauliflower, pak choi and kale – contain sulphur-based chemicals called glucosinolates that help rid the body of harmful substances, such as pollutants and toxic metals. These can build up in the reproductive system of both men and women and may reduce your chances of fertility. Glucosinolates also promote balance between the female sex hormones oestrogen and progesterone, which support a healthy menstrual cycle and a woman's chances of conception. Add in vitamin C, vitamin E and the carotenoids lutein and beta carotene for antioxidant protection against damage to egg and sperm, and broccoli provides you with the full cleansing package. The high levels of folate (folic acid) also help prevent birth defects and premature birth.

- Contains glucosinolates and fibre that remove harmful, anti-fertility substances from the body.
- Sulphur compounds also balance hormones for conception.
- Contains high levels of protective antioxidants that prevent damage to both egg and sperm.
- Provides folate, needed in preparation for a healthy, full-term pregnancy.

Practical tips:
To preserve both the taste and nutrients of broccoli, steam or lightly stir-fry, and be careful not to overcook. Try different varieties and enjoy broccoli simply, with olive oil and lemon juice.

DID YOU KNOW?
The strong green colour of broccoli is proof of the concentrated amounts of chlorophyll used by the plant to trap energy from the sun. Chlorophyll has long been used by traditional healers to 'nourish the blood', thereby promoting fertility.

MAJOR NUTRIENTS PER 100 G/3½ OZ BROCCOLI

Kcalories	34
Total fat	0.37 g
Protein	2.82 g
Carbohydrate	6.64 g
Fibre	2.6 g
Vitamin C	89.2 mg
Vitamin A	623 IU
Vitamin E	0.78 mg
Folate	90 mcg
Beta carotene	361 mcg
Lutein/Zeaxanthin	1,121 mcg

Broccoli and mangetout stir-fry

SERVES 4   (G) (A) (V) (Q)

2 tbsp vegetable or groundnut oil

1 garlic clove, finely chopped

225 g/8 oz small florets broccoli

115 g/4 oz mangetout, trimmed

225 g/8 oz Chinese leaves, cut into
    1-cm/½-inch slices

5–6 spring onions, finely chopped

2 tbsp light soy sauce

1 tsp sesame oil

1 tsp sesame seeds, lightly toasted

Method

1 In a preheated wok, heat the oil then add the garlic and stir-fry for
30 seconds. Add all the vegetables and stir-fry over a high heat for
3 minutes.

2 Pour in the soy sauce and sesame oil and cook for a further minute.
Sprinkle with the sesame seeds and serve hot.

05

CAULIFLOWER

Like its other cruciferous cousins, cauliflower contains sulphur compounds that support detoxification and help balance female hormones ready for conception.

As one of the cruciferous vegetables, along with broccoli, cabbage, kale, pak choi and Brussels sprouts, cauliflower contains the chemical di-indolylmethane (DIM), which may help your body use oestrogen more efficiently and support the chances of fertility. Cauliflower is one of the important foods to include in a fertility diet to help the liver process and eliminate toxins that may interfere with reproduction. The antioxidant vitamin C increases the effect of other antioxidants consumed to support detoxification. Vitamin C also supports the immune system to protect against infectious bacteria that may affect fertility. Cauliflower also contains the two B vitamins folate (folic acid) and choline, which together help protect against the likelihood of spina bifida or neural tube defect in the embryo.

- DIM helps utilize oestrogen to the best advantage for pregnancy to occur.
- Sulphur compounds and vitamin C support detoxification and immunity to optimize fertility.
- Folate and choline work together to help lessen the risk of neural tube defect.

Practical tips:
Cauliflower can suffer from overcooking and become mushy; to avoid this, stir-fry rather than boil or steam. While boiling cauliflower for longer than five minutes has shown a significant reduction in nutrients, these are retained well when steaming or stir-frying.

DID YOU KNOW?

Cauliflower works very well in curries, and particularly with the anti-inflammatory and detoxifying spice turmeric for a great fertility combination to prepare your body for conception.

MAJOR NUTRIENTS PER 100 G/3½ OZ CAULIFLOWER

Kcalories	25
Total fat	0.28 g
Protein	1.92 g
Carbohydrate	4.97 g
Fibre	2.0 g
Vitamin C	48.2 mg
Vitamin K	28.5 mcg
Folate	57 mcg
Choline	44.3 mg
Potassium	299 mg

Cauliflower soup

SERVES 6   (G) (A) (V)

1 tbsp olive oil
25 g/1 oz butter
1 large onion, coarsely chopped
2 leeks, sliced
1 large cauliflower
900 ml/1½ pints vegetable stock
salt and pepper
finely grated Cheddar cheese and
   extra virgin olive oil, to serve

Method

1 Heat the oil and butter in a large saucepan and fry the onion and leeks for 10 minutes, stirring frequently, taking care not to allow the vegetables to colour.

2 Cut the cauliflower into florets and cut the stalk into small pieces. Add to the pan and sauté with the other vegetables for 2–3 minutes.

3 Add the stock and bring to the boil, cover and simmer over a medium heat for 20 minutes.

4 Pour the soup into a food processor or blender, process until smooth and return to the rinsed-out saucepan. Heat the soup through, season to taste with salt and pepper and serve in warmed soup bowls topped with a spoonful of grated cheese and a drizzle of extra virgin olive oil.

06 BUCKWHEAT

Buckwheat provides a rich helping of the B vitamins and magnesium vital for energy, sex drive and fertility. Any food that can give these a boost is one to remember!

B vitamins and magnesium are needed to produce energy in our cells, making them essential to the creation of new life. In addition, they help us cope with stress – anxiety has been shown to be a major barrier to conception. Buckwheat is also a very good source of slow-release energy, so its inclusion in the diet helps prevent the blood sugar highs and lows that can rob would-be parents of the energy needed for procreation. It is an excellent source of rutin, a circulation-boosting antioxidant that carries blood supply, energy and nutrients to the reproductive areas. These areas are further protected by the cleansing capacity of buckwheat, along with its zinc and selenium content, which can help prevent damage caused by pollution, harmful chemicals and some medications. Zinc and selenium are very often found to be low in women and men who are infertile.

- B vitamins and magnesium help keep up energy levels and combat stress, which can interfere with fertility.
- Contains rutin, which supports circulation and therefore blood and oxygen flow to reproductive areas.
- Antioxidants zinc and selenium support fertility levels and prevent damage by environmental toxins.

Practical tips:
Use buckwheat flour to make pancakes. Buckwheat is often found in wheat-free products, but its lack of gluten means it doesn't produce the 'fluffiness' considered desirable in many breads.

DID YOU KNOW?

Buckwheat is actually a fruit seed and much easier to digest than a grain. As such, it is less likely to cause any intolerance or inflammation that may interfere with your chances of fertility.

MAJOR NUTRIENTS PER 100 G/3½ OZ BUCKWHEAT

Kcalories	343
Total fat	3.4 g
Omega-6 fatty acids	1,052 mg
Protein	13.25 g
Carbohydrate	71.5 g
Fibre	10 g
Vitamin B2	0.43 mg
Vitamin B3	7.02 mg
Vitamin B5	1.23 mg
Vitamin B6	0.21 mg
Magnesium	231 g
Potassium	460 mg
Manganese	1.33 mg
Selenium	8.3 g
Zinc	2.4 mg

Buckwheat crêpes

MAKES 10 (A) (V) (Q)

350 g/12 oz buckwheat flour
pinch of sea salt (optional)
400 ml/14 fl oz milk
about 250 ml/9 fl oz water
about 70 g/2½ oz butter, melted
2 tsp olive oil
cherry tomatoes, to serve

Filling

200 g/7 oz ricotta cheese
4 large chargrilled red peppers in
    olive oil, drained and thinly sliced
3 tbsp chopped fresh basil
pepper

Method

1 Sift the flour and salt into a large mixing bowl, then make a well in the centre. Add half of the milk and gradually stir into the flour to make a thick, smooth batter. Gradually beat in the remaining milk. Cover the bowl with clingfilm and set aside to rest for 45 minutes.

2 Uncover the batter and beat in 150 ml/5 fl oz water, then slowly beat in more water until the batter is the consistency of single cream. Add half of the butter and beat until incorporated.

3 Heat a 23-cm/9-inch non-stick frying pan over a medium–high heat until very hot. Add the oil and swirl the pan until it coats the surface. Reduce the heat to medium. Rub the surface of the pan with a little of the remaining butter. Drop a small ladleful of batter in the centre of the pan and immediately lift and tip the pan so the batter covers the base as thinly as possible. Cook the crêpe until it is golden brown with holes starting to appear on the surface, then flip it over, using a palette knife. Cook until the other side is set, then transfer to a plate and keep warm. Repeat until all the batter is used.

4 Arrange the crêpes on the work surface, then divide the ricotta, red peppers and basil between them. Season with pepper and turn the sides of each crêpe into the centre, then fold in at the ends to make a square package.

5 Reheat the pan. Rub with the remaining butter, add the crêpes, folded side down, and cook for 90 seconds, then flip over and cook for a further 30 seconds, or until the crêpes are hot and the filling warmed through. Serve hot, garnished with the cherry tomatoes.

07 GUAVA

The antioxidants in guava protect every part of the body from free radical damage. This damage can penetrate our DNA, and affect our ability to reproduce.

Free radicals come from sunlight, pollution, fried food, and even the essential process of creating energy. Free radical damage occurs in every part of our body all the time, and we need a constant and varied supply of antioxidants to stop it causing harm, and to protect the egg and sperm from damage. The fibre in guava also carries toxins out of the body. Guava is especially supportive of sperm health, as vitamin C increases the number of sperm produced, beta carotene boosts their concentration, vitamin E aids their ability to travel, and zinc improves their quality. All of these antioxidants protect the egg, too, and make it ripe for fertilization. The zinc in guava aids normal foetal development, and the antioxidant proanthocyanidins, which helps to make the guava flesh red, encourages a healthy flow of blood to the penis.

- High antioxidant levels and fibre protect both egg and sperm from the free radical damage that naturally occurs every day.
- Contains a range of nutrients, including vitamins C and E, that help create healthy sperm, able to travel to and fertilize the egg.
- Proanthocyanidins support blood flow to the male reproductive area, enabling sexual function.

Practical tips:
When selecting guavas, avoid any that are spotty, mushy or very green and choose those that are yellowish in colour and that yield slightly when pressed. Eat on its own as a snack, or use as any other fruit; try it juiced, in salads or with cereal.

DID YOU KNOW?

The red flesh of the guava is the clue to the rich fat-soluble antioxidants it contains. Lycopene, beta carotene and vitamin E all help to support the environment in which sperm are stored and carried.

MAJOR NUTRIENTS PER MEDIUM-SIZED GUAVA

Kcalories	37
Total fat	0.52 g
Protein	1.4 g
Carbohydrate	7.88 g
Fibre	3 g
Vitamin C	125.6 mg
Vitamin E	0.4 mg
Zinc	0.13 mg
Beta carotene	206 mcg
Lycopene	2,862 mcg

Guava smoothie

SERVES 2   Ⓖ Ⓐ Ⓥ Ⓠ

400 g/14 oz canned guavas,
*   drained*
225ml/8 fl oz ice-cold milk

Method

1 Place the guavas in a food processor or blender and pour
   in the milk.
2 Process until well blended.
3 Strain into glasses to remove the hard seeds. Serve.

08

LAMB

Lamb is a dense, quality-protein meat with a useful vitamin-B profile. Consumed in moderation, it can help the body make the structures and cells necessary for fertility.

MAJOR NUTRIENTS PER 100 G/3½ OZ LAMB

Kcalories	229
Total fat	16.97 g
Saturated fat	8.18 g
Monounsaturated fat	6.91 g
Protein	17.84 g
Carbohydrate	0 g
Fibre	0 g
Vitamin B2	0.26 mg
Vitamin B3	4.93 mg
Vitamin B5	0.56 mg
Vitamin B6	0.34 mg
Vitamin B12	2.47 mcg
Iron	1.43 mg
Zinc	3.67 mg
Selenium	7.5 mcg

Lamb provides all nine of the amino acids, the protein building blocks necessary for healthy sperm, womb lining and cell replication, as well as the B vitamins needed to make these new proteins. It also contains good levels of the antioxidant trace minerals selenium and zinc, which protect the egg, sperm and uterus from damage and help the liver remove the toxins that can interfere with reproductive processes. Zinc deficiency has been linked to infertility and miscarriage, because zinc is needed for all body tissues and organisms to grow. Lamb also provides another antioxidant, coenzyme-Q10, that may help conception by improving blood supply and energy in cells within the reproductive organs.

- A quality protein that also contains B vitamins, promoting a healthy uterus, sperm, and efficient cell division, all of which encourages chances of conception.
- Contains the antioxidants zinc and selenium that protect the reproductive organs from damage.
- Coenzyme-Q10 content supports a healthy blood supply and energy within the reproductive system.

Practical tips:

Lamb contains high levels of saturated fat so do not eat more than once a week. Chops are the healthiest cuts. Choose free-range, organic lamb, if possible, to ensure the best quality fats and minimum levels of damaging hormones and chemicals.

Stir-fried lamb with orange

SERVES 4 (G)(A)(Q)

1 tbsp vegetable or groundnut oil
450 g/1 lb minced lamb
2 cloves garlic, crushed
1 tsp cumin seeds
1 tsp ground coriander
1 red onion, finely sliced
grated rind and juice of 1 orange
2 tbsp soy sauce
1 orange, peeled and segmented
pepper
snipped fresh chives, to garnish

Method

1 Heat a wok or large, non-stick frying pan. Add the oil and lamb and stir-fry for 5 minutes or until evenly browned. Drain away any excess fat from the wok.

2 Add the garlic, cumin seeds, coriander and red onion to the wok and stir-fry for a further 5 minutes.

3 Stir in the orange rind and juice and the soy sauce, mixing until thoroughly combined. Cover, reduce the heat and simmer, stirring occasionally, for 15 minutes.

4 Remove the lid, increase the heat and add the orange segments. Stir to mix.

5 Season with pepper and heat through for a further 2–3 minutes. Serve immediately, garnished with chives.

09 MILK

Milk provides a complete protein source, supplying the building blocks needed for conception, to make new sperm and a healthy womb lining.

This versatile food is particularly good for vegetarians, who do not have many other sources of complete protein in their diet. Milk also supplies the body with the macro-minerals calcium, potassium and phosphorus, which are needed in large amounts for a growing baby's skeleton. A lack of these minerals in the mother can increase a baby's risk of growth and development problems and impaired muscular function, so it is important to keep up maternal intake. Increasing calcium intake before pregnancy has been shown to reduce risk of hypertension (high blood pressure), and the related complication pre-eclampsia, later in pregnancy.

- A complete protein that is suitable for vegetarians, which enables the body to create sperm and the new cells needed for reproduction.
- Helps the expectant mother stock up on calcium, potassium and phosphorus in anticipation of the baby's bone growth and development.
- Calcium helps reduce the risk of high blood pressure developing later in pregnancy.

Practical tips:
You won't get the goodness of milk by using it in tea or coffee, because the potentially damaging effects of caffeine outweigh its benefits. Enjoy it on cereal or in a smoothie, and don't overdo milk consumption if you tend to get nasal or digestive problems.

DID YOU KNOW?
Choosing organic milk will reduce the amount of hormones and antibiotics you take into your body. These are regularly added to the feed of cows on non-organic farms, and can interfere with the ability to conceive.

MAJOR NUTRIENTS PER 100 ML/3½ FL OZ SEMI-SKIMMED MILK

Kcalories	50
Total fat	3.33 g
Protein	3.33 g
Carbohydrate	6.66 g
Vitamin D	43.66 IU
Betaine	1 mg
Choline	16.66 mg
Calcium	119 mg
Potassium	152.66 mg

Spiced banana milkshake

SERVES 2 (G) (A) (V) (Q)

350 ml/12 fl oz milk

2 bananas

150 ml/5 fl oz natural bio yogurt

½ tsp mixed spice, and a pinch of
    mixed spice, to decorate

6 ice cubes (optional)

Method

1 Place the milk, bananas, yogurt and mixed spice in a food
  processor or blender and process gently until smooth.

2 Pour the mixture into two glasses and serve with ice, if using.
  Add a pinch of mixed spice to decorate.

10

SUN-DRIED TOMATOES

The antioxidants in sun-dried tomatoes are mainly fat-soluble, which means they protect fatty areas of the body, including the reproductive organs, eggs and sperm.

Lycopene and other fat-soluble antioxidant carotenoids, such as beta carotene, lutein and zeaxanthin, are found in large concentrations in healthy testes. Lycopene has been shown to support male fertility, particularly as it plays a part in correcting low sperm count and even abnormal sperm. Tomatoes, or other deep, rich coloured vegetables, need to be eaten daily in order to keep these antioxidant levels up and capable of protecting healthy sperm from damage. The essential minerals sodium and potassium are also provided in good amounts by this fruit, keeping our bodies alkalized and hydrated, and ensuring the efficient removal of toxins that may prevent conception.

- Lycopene is particularly important for ensuring good levels of healthy, active sperm.
- Contain fat-soluble carotenoids that ensure the male testes are the best possible breeding ground for sperm.
- The right balance of sodium and potassium ensures the removal of toxins that can affect fertility.

Practical tips:
The table of major nutrients on this page refers only to the dried tomatoes themselves, but you can receive extra benefits by eating sun-dried tomatoes that are sold in a good quality extra virgin olive oil. The oil provides oleic acid to move the essential fatty acids and carotenoids that help to keep us fertile into our cells.

MAJOR NUTRIENTS PER 100 G /3½ OZ SUN-DRIED TOMATOES, WITHOUT OIL

Kcalories	258
Total fat	2.97 g
Protein	14.11 g
Carbohydrate	55.76 g
Fibre	12.3 g
Vitamin C	39.2 mg
Vitamin A	874 IU
Magnesium	194 mg
Potassium	3,427 mg
Sodium	2,095 mg
Lycopene	45,902 mcg
Beta carotene	524 mcg
Lutein/Zeaxanthin	1,419 mcg

Asparagus and sun-dried tomato risotto

SERVES 4   (A)

1 litre/1¾ pints vegetable stock
1 tbsp olive oil
40 g/1½ oz butter
1 small onion, finely chopped
6 sun-dried tomatoes, thinly sliced
280 g/10 oz risotto rice
150 ml/5 fl oz alcohol-free dry
    white wine
225 g/8 oz fresh asparagus spears,
    cooked
pepper
freshly grated Parmesan or Grana
    Padano cheese and finely
    grated lemon rind, to serve

Method

1 Bring the stock to the boil in a saucepan, then reduce the heat and simmer over a low heat while you cook the risotto.

2 Heat the oil with 25 g/1 oz of the butter in a deep saucepan over a medium heat until the butter has melted. Stir in the onion and sun-dried tomatoes, and cook, stirring occasionally, for 5 minutes, until the onion is soft and starting to turn golden. Do not brown.

3 Reduce the heat, add the rice and mix to coat it in oil and butter. Cook, stirring constantly, for 2–3 minutes, or until the grains are translucent. Add the wine and cook, stirring constantly, until reduced.

4 Gradually add the hot stock, a ladleful at a time. Stir constantly and add more liquid as the rice absorbs each addition. Increase the heat to medium so that the liquid bubbles. Cook for 20 minutes, or until all the liquid is absorbed and the rice is creamy. Season with pepper, to taste.

5 While the risotto is cooking, cut most of the asparagus (set aside 4 spears to garnish) into 2.5-cm/1-inch long pieces. Carefully fold the sliced asparagus into the risotto for the last 5 minutes of cooking time.

6 Remove the risotto from the heat and add the remaining butter. Mix well. Spoon the risotto into warmed serving dishes and garnish with the reserved asparagus. Sprinkle some Parmesan and lemon rind on top then serve.

11

QUINOA

Quinoa provides all of the essential amino acids needed to make proteins, which are crucial for reproduction. It also has a rich mineral and B-vitamin content.

MAJOR NUTRIENTS PER 100 G/3½ OZ UNCOOKED QUINOA

Kcalories	368
Total fat	6.07 g
Omega-6 fatty acids	2,977 mg
Protein	14.12 g
Carbohydrate	64.16 g
Fibre	7 g
Vitamin B1	0.36 mg
Vitamin B2	0.32 mg
Vitamin B3	1.52 mg
Vitamin B5	0.77 mg
Vitamin B6	0.49 mg
Folate	184 mcg
Magnesium	197 mg
Iron	4.57 mg
Manganese	2.03 mg
Selenium	8.5 mcg
Zinc	3.1 mg

Low protein levels can interfere with the frequency of the menstrual cycle and also the quality of sperm, both of which can lead to lower chances of conception. This complete protein from the plant kingdom is more alkalizing than animal sources of protein, so it helps maintain the slightly alkaline environment needed for a healthy egg and womb. This environment is also vital in the male reproductive system, in order for sperm to flourish and then be able to travel and fertilize the egg inside the woman. Omega-6 fatty acids keep all the cells concerned supple and intact and, along with the B vitamins, maintain the balance of female and male sex hormones necessary for conception. The folate (folic acid) and zinc in quinoa also work together to allow reproduction to occur and prepare the body for a healthy full-term pregnancy.

• Complete protein that supports healthy periods and sperm.
• Contains omega-6 fatty acids and the B vitamins to support sex hormone levels in both women and men.
• Folate and zinc combine to enable the new cell production needed for conception.

Practical tips:
Quinoa can be used like a grain but is actually a seed, which makes it very easy on the digestion. It soaks up other flavours well and can be used as a salad base or a sweet porridge with fruit. For a protein boost, you can also try adding it to smoothies.

Quinoa and walnut tabbouleh

SERVES 2 ⓖ ⓥ ⓠ

100 g/3½ oz quinoa
250 ml/9 fl oz water
1 courgette, coarsely grated
2 large spring onions, thinly sliced
   diagonally
handful fresh mint leaves, chopped
handful fresh flat-leaf parsley
   leaves, chopped
8 walnut halves, chopped

Dressing
3 tbsp extra virgin olive oil
1 tbsp lemon juice
1 tsp Dijon mustard
1 garlic clove, crushed
pepper

Method

1 Put the quinoa in a saucepan and pour over the water. Bring to
   the boil, reduce the heat to its lowest setting, cover with a lid, and
   simmer for about 15 minutes, until the water has been absorbed
   and the grains are tender. Set aside, covered, for 5 minutes.

2 Transfer the quinoa to a bowl and add the courgette, spring onions,
   mint and parsley.

3 Mix together the ingredients for the dressing then pour over the
   tabbouleh. Turn gently until combined.

4 Sprinkle with the walnuts just before serving at room temperature.

12 RADISH

Radish helps balance hormones and detoxify the body. The chemical raphanin supports thyroid health, helping would-be parents maintain energy levels.

All of the cruciferous vegetables provide sulphur compounds, such as glucosinolates, that balance oestrogen and progesterone in women, enabling healthy ovulation and fertilization, and later the ability to support the growing foetus in the womb. Radish comes with the added bonus of supporting the thyroid gland, which plays a part in regulating these hormones over the course of the menstrual cycle. Glucosinolates also help remove xenoestrogens from the body; found in plastics and tap water, these can mimic and disrupt our body's natural hormones. The folate (folic acid) and calcium in radish further prepare the body to support a healthy foetus and take it to full term in a successful pregnancy.

- Sulphur-containing glucosinolates optimize the balance of hormones prior to pregnancy, and help remove xenoestrogens, which can interfere with this balance.
- Contains raphanin, which supports thyroid health, providing energy for procreation and reproduction, and helping to regulate sex hormones.
- Guards against folate and calcium deficiencies that can have a detrimental effect on fertility and jeopardize pregnancy.

Practical tips:
Add radishes to salads – their sharp, crisp taste will help the digestive juices flow. They can also be added to juices. Try more exotic varieties if available, such as daikon.

DID YOU KNOW?

If you are prone to constipation, limit your chances of developing haemorrhoids in pregnancy by eating radishes now. Vitamin C, fibre and liver support will help prevent toxic build-up in the colon and heal tissues.

MAJOR NUTRIENTS PER 2 RADISHES

Kcalories	2
Total fat	0 g
Protein	0.06 g
Carbohydrate	0.30 g
Fibre	0.2 g
Vitamin C	1.4 mg
Folate	2 mcg
Potassium	20 mg
Calcium	2 mg

Chicken and radish salad

SERVES 2 (G) (A) (N)

2 skinless, boneless chicken
    breasts, about 175 g/6 oz each
2 tbsp olive oil
2 tsp dried thyme
2 tsp ground coriander
100 g/3½ oz frozen soya beans
1 small Little Gem lettuce, leaves
    separated
55 g/2 oz mangetout, sliced
    diagonally
1 large spring onion, thinly sliced
    diagonally
5 radishes, sliced into rounds
pepper

Dressing

handful fresh mint leaves
6 tbsp natural bio yogurt
juice of ½ lime
½ tsp cumin seeds
pepper

Method

1 Using a meat mallet or the end of a rolling pin, flatten the chicken until about 1 cm/½ inch thick. Pour the olive oil into a large, shallow bowl and stir in the thyme and coriander. Season with pepper and add the chicken and turn until coated.

2 Heat a griddle pan over a medium–high heat. Griddle the chicken for 6 minutes, turning once, until cooked through and golden.

3 Meanwhile, cook the soya beans in a little boiling water for 3–4 minutes, or until tender. Drain and refresh under cold running water.

4 Using a food processor or blender, mix together the first three ingredients for the dressing. Transfer to a bowl, season with pepper and scatter over the cumin seeds.

5 Divide the lettuce leaves between two large, shallow bowls then top with the mangetout, spring onion, radishes and soya beans. Slice the chicken lengthways and arrange on top of the salad. Spoon the dressing over before serving.

13 MACKEREL

Mackerel provides essential omega-3 fatty acids, which ensure the correct fat balance in the cells of sperm, egg and womb. These also help to balance female sex hormones.

It is difficult to underestimate the importance of omega-3 fatty acids in our diets in terms of supporting fertility and also the developing brain of the foetus. In mackerel, and other oily fish, these fatty acids take the form of DHA (docosahexaenoic acid) and EPA (eicosapentaenoic acid) and help to balance out any excess of omega-6 fatty acids, which our bodies take in the modern diet from grains and nuts. DHA and EPA help us cope with stress, too, through the production of the 'happy' brain chemicals serotonin and dopamine, which support libido. Stress reduction is a key component in addressing fertility issues. The high protein and B-vitamin levels in mackerel add to the stress-reducing effect, by helping to balance blood sugar and create the energy needed for reproduction.

- Omega-3 fatty acids DHA and EPA support reproductive systems and balance out the hormones needed to make these work.
- Omega-3 fatty acids also support healthy sexual function.
- Omega-3 fatty acids, alongside protein and B vitamins, help reduce stress reactions and boost energy levels ready for fertility.

Practical tips:
Mackerel is one of the safer oily fish to eat as it contains very low levels of mercury, which is shown to directly affect fertility in both men and women. However, do not eat it more than twice a week during pregnancy, and avoid king mackerel entirely.

DID YOU KNOW?
Some scientists believe that it was our ancestors' consumption of oily fish that contributed to the human brain developing the conscious and cognitive thought processes that we take for granted today.

MAJOR NUTRIENTS PER 100 G/3½ OZ FRESH MACKEREL

Kcalories	105
Total fat	2 g
Omega-3 fatty acids – EPA	0.136 g
Omega-3 fatty acids – DHA	0.18 g
Protein	20.28 g
Vitamin B3	8.6 mg
Vitamin A	727 IU

Spiced mackerel with tomato salad

SERVES 4　Ⓖ Ⓐ Ⓠ

4 garlic cloves, crushed

finely grated zest and juice of
　1 lemon

1 heaped tsp ground cumin

1 heaped tsp smoked paprika

2–3 tbsp olive oil

4 large mackerel fillets, about
　200 g/7 oz each, or 8 small,
　about 100 g/3½ oz each

Tomato salad

300 g/10½ oz juicy ripe tomatoes,
　sliced

1 small red onion, thinly sliced

1 heaped tbsp chopped fresh
　herbs, such as thyme, mint
　or parsley

2 tbsp olive oil

1 tbsp white wine vinegar

pepper

Method

1　Mix together the garlic, lemon zest and juice, cumin, paprika and
　oil in a small bowl. Put the mackerel fillets in a shallow, non-metallic
　dish and thoroughly rub both sides with the spice mixture. Cover
　and leave to marinate in a cool place for 30 minutes, if possible.

2　Preheat the grill to high. Lay the mackerel fillets in the grill pan
　and cook under the preheated grill for 3 minutes on one side, then
　turn over, drizzle with any remaining marinade and cook for
　a further 2–3 minutes, or until the mackerel is cooked through.

3　Meanwhile, prepare the tomato salad. Arrange the tomatoes and
　onion on a serving platter. Put the herbs, oil and vinegar in a screw-
　top jar and shake well to combine. Season with pepper, to taste.

4　Drizzle the dressing over the tomato salad and serve with the hot
　mackerel fillets.

14

CORIANDER LEAF

Coriander leaves have been shown to remove toxic metals from our bodies. The absence of these metals quickly improves chances of conception.

Heavy metal toxicity, even at low levels, can affect men and women profoundly. Mercury from fillings, tuna and vaccinations has been most frequently associated with female infertility. Male infertility has been predominantly linked to lead, found in pollution, cigarette smoke and old pipes. Toxic metals can hide in the reproductive organs and, as such, not affect our day-to-day bodily systems. The antioxidant nutrients vitamins A and C and carotenoids beta carotene, lutein and zeaxanthin in coriander support the plant's ability to remove toxic metals by protecting the cells and tissues they can harm. Coriander has also been shown to protect calcium levels in the body by reducing the lead build-up in bone.

- Effectively and safely removes toxic metals, such as mercury and lead, that are linked to female and male infertility.
- High antioxidant levels protect the body tissues as toxic metals leave the body.
- Helps restore calcium levels in bone by removing lead.
- The fragrant volatile oils are antimicrobials that help destroy immune-stressing invaders.

Practical tips:
Add fresh coriander to salads, and use to garnish soups, stews and curries, just before serving, to preserve the nutrients. Add a handful to a juice or smoothie or create a simple pesto by adding a few chopped teaspoons to Brazil nuts, olive oil and garlic.

DID YOU KNOW?

The fragrant smell of coriander leaves heralds the potency of their pungent oils. As strong antimicrobial agents, these oils ward off infections that can interfere with conception.

MAJOR NUTRIENTS PER 15 G/½ OZ CORIANDER LEAF

Kcalories	3.45
Total fat	0.08 g
Protein	0.32 g
Carbohydrate	0.55 g
Fibre	0.42 g
Vitamin C	4.05 mg
Vitamin A	1,012.2 IU
Vitamin K	46.5 mcg
Beta carotene	589.5 mcg
Lutein/Zeaxanthin	129.75 mcg

Turkey skewers with coriander pesto

SERVES 4 (A) (N)

450 g/1 lb skinless, boneless
    turkey, cut into 5-cm/2-inch
    cubes
2 courgettes, thickly sliced
1 red and 1 yellow pepper,
    deseeded and cut into
    5-cm/2-inch squares
8 cherry tomatoes
8 baby onions, peeled but left
    whole

Marinade
4 tbsp olive oil
2 tsp Dijon mustard
1 tsp green peppercorns, crushed
2 tbsp chopped fresh coriander

Coriander pesto
55 g/2 oz fresh coriander leaves
15 g/½ oz fresh parsley leaves
1 garlic clove
55 g/2 oz pine kernels
25 g/1 oz Parmesan cheese,
    freshly grated
6 tbsp extra virgin olive oil
juice of 1 lemon

Method

1 Place the turkey in a large bowl. To make the marinade, mix the olive oil, mustard, peppercorns and coriander together in a jug. Pour the mixture over the turkey and turn until the turkey is thoroughly coated. Cover with clingfilm and leave to marinate in the refrigerator for 2 hours.

2 Preheat the grill to medium–high. To make the coriander pesto, put the coriander and parsley into a food processor and process until finely chopped. Add the garlic and pine kernels and pulse until chopped. Add the Parmesan, oil and lemon juice and process briefly to mix. Transfer to a bowl, cover and leave to chill in the refrigerator until required.

3 Thread the turkey (reserving the marinade), courgettes, peppers, cherry tomatoes and onions alternately onto pre-soaked wooden skewers. Grill under a medium–high heat, turning and brushing frequently with the marinade, for 10–12 minutes. Serve immediately with the coriander pesto.

15 CINNAMON

Cinnamon is a powerful spice and a traditional aphrodisiac. It also helps reduce cravings for sweet foods that rob us of the nutrients we need for reproduction.

The active compound in cinnamon, methylhydroxychalcone polymer (MHCP), acts in the same way as the hormone insulin, taking sugars from dietary sources from the bloodstream into our cells to be used as energy. Eating too many refined sugars in the form of cakes, biscuits and sweets causes sudden surges of sugar into the bloodstream and sets up a cycle of sugar highs and lows, whereby the body regularly craves sugar and often caffeine in order to pull itself out of an energy slump. Just half a teaspoon of cinnamon per day has been shown to decrease excess blood sugar and put an end to these cravings. Cinnamon is also a strong antioxidant and works hard to protect the body from damage.

- Contains the substance MHCP, which evens out blood sugar levels and supports a sustained release of energy.
- Breaks the cycles of dependence on sugar, caffeine and other stimulants that undermine fertility.
- Its powerful antioxidant properties help prevent and even repair damage caused by excess dietary sugars.

Practical tips:
Powdered cinnamon spice is stronger than the stick form, but it does not stay fresh for as long – replace when the characteristic smell has faded. Cinnamon naturally sweetens food, so add to juices, porridge, yogurt or cereal. Do not take supplements or consume cinnamon in large amounts during pregnancy.

DID YOU KNOW?
In traditional Chinese medicine, cinnamon is used to treat infertility by increasing male yang energy, and by increasing blood flow to the reproductive organs in both sexes.

MAJOR NUTRIENTS PER 15 G/½ OZ GROUND CINNAMON (CASSIA)

Kcalories	37
Total fat	0.19 g
Protein	0.59 g
Carbohydrate	12.09 g
Fibre	7.97 g
Vitamin C	0.57 mg
Vitamin A	44.25 IU
Calcium	150.3 mg
Manganese	2.62 mg

Cinnamon, apple and blackberry crunch

SERVES 2 (A) (N) (V) (Q)

2 dessert apples, peeled, cored
   and diced

75 ml/2½ fl oz water

50 g/1¾ oz jumbo oats

1 tsp ground cinnamon, plus extra
   for sprinkling

3 tsp clear honey

115 g/4 oz blackberries

250 g/9 oz Greek-style bio yogurt

2 tbsp flaked almonds

Method

1 Put the apples in a saucepan and stew in the water, covered, for 10–12 minutes, until tender. Mash with the back of a fork or potato masher to make a coarse purée.

2 Meanwhile, toast the oats in a large, dry, non-stick frying pan for 5 minutes, tossing regularly, until light golden. Remove from the pan and leave to cool.

3 When the apples are cooked, stir in the cinnamon, 2 teaspoons of the honey and the blackberries.

4 To serve, put a quarter of the oats in each of 2 large wine glasses or bowls. Top each with quarter of the yogurt then half of the fruit mixture, followed by half of the remaining yogurt. Divide the rest of the oats, scatter over the tops and drizzle with the honey. To finish, sprinkle with a little extra cinnamon and the almonds.

16 MISO

In Japanese culture, miso has a long association with female health and fertility. Most Japanese include it in the diet several times a week.

Miso is made by fermenting soya beans. In common with other traditional fermented food, such as yogurt, it can help support the immune and digestive systems, which keeps bacteria from causing harm and interfering with fertility. Miso also contains a plant form of oestrogen that cleverly adjusts the levels in our body if they are too high or too low. This effect can be thrown out of balance, however, if too much is eaten. Miso also contains vitamin K, which is needed to transport calcium to our bones. A prospective mother needs to ensure she has optimum levels of calcium before pregnancy so that her stores don't get depleted by the growing baby's skeleton.

- A fermented food that supports good digestion and encourages our immune system to ward off harmful infections.
- A plant form of oestrogen that can help correct sex hormone imbalances when eaten a few times a week.
- Contains vitamin K, which helps calcium to mineralize into bone in preparation for good mother and baby bone health.

Practical tips:
The commonest form of miso (hatcho) is made from soya beans and this has the highest hormone-balancing effect. If you are intolerant to soya, try rice, barley or wheat misos. The paste form is far superior to the powder. Make a simple miso soup by boiling dark leafy greens lightly in water and adding paste to taste. Miso is high in sodium so use in moderation.

DID YOU KNOW?

Although soya products have been the subject of controversy, natural, fermented soya foods such as miso and tempeh have been shown to support fertility.

MAJOR NUTRIENTS PER 15 ML/1 TBSP MISO

Kcalories	34
Total fat	1.03 g
Protein	2.01 g
Carbohydrate	4.55 g
Fibre	0.93 g
Vitamin B1	0.02 mg
Vitamin B2	0.04 mg
Vitamin B3	0.16 mg
Vitamin B5	0.06 mg
Vitamin B6	0.03 mg
Vitamin B12	0.01 mcg
Vitamin K	4.98 mcg
Iron	0.43 mg
Selenium	1.2 mcg
Zinc	0.44 mg

Miso fish soup

SERVES 4 (**G**)(**A**)(**N**)(**Q**)

850 ml/1½ pints fish stock or
    vegetable stock

2.5-cm/1-inch piece fresh ginger,
    peeled and grated

1 tbsp fish sauce

1 fresh chilli, deseeded and finely
    sliced

1 carrot, thinly sliced

55 g/2 oz daikon, cut into thin
    strips or ½ bunch radishes,
    trimmed and sliced

1 yellow pepper, deseeded and cut
    into thin strips

85 g/3 oz shiitake mushrooms,
    sliced if large

40 g/1½ oz thread egg noodles

225 g/8 oz sole fillets, skinned and
    cut into strips

1 tbsp miso paste

4 spring onions, trimmed and
    shredded

Method

1 Pour the stock into a large saucepan and add the ginger, fish sauce
and chilli. Bring to the boil then reduce the heat and simmer for
5 minutes.

2 Add the carrot with the daikon, pepper, mushrooms and noodles
and simmer for a further 3 minutes.

3 Add the fish strips with the miso paste and continue to cook
for 2 minutes, or until the fish is tender. Divide equally between
4 warmed soup bowls, top with the spring onions and serve.

17 PEARS

Pears, like apples, contain good amounts of the soluble fibre pectin, known to help protect the body from environmental toxins that may affect fertility.

Pectin is a helpful regulator for bowel activity, a useful tool to support other body functions necessary for fertility. As it attracts toxins that enter the body through food and also binds to those being eliminated through the liver, it may help prevent toxic metals such as mercury and lead entering the blood circulation where they can affect the reproductive system. Pectin is mildly diuretic and laxative, and works with insoluble fibre to clean out your bowels regularly. Healthy bowel function can help support correct female hormone balance and pectin also has prebiotic action; its fibre feeds our beneficial probiotic or healthy bowel bacteria which help regulate levels of oestrogen and progesterone to prepare for conception.

- The soluble fibre pectin removes toxins that may reduce the chances of conception.
- Pectin and insoluble fibre help regulate bowel function to further support detoxification.
- Pectin feeds healthy bacteria for the correct female hormone balance needed for fertility.

Practical tips:
You need to eat the skins of pears to benefit from the cleansing insoluble fibre. Eat like an apple or stew them with some cinnamon. Pears are often included in diets for those with food sensitivities because they are known to be hypoallergenic.

DID YOU KNOW?

Pears make the perfect sweet snack, because the pectin they contain slows down the rate at which your body absorbs the sugars present in them. This is the opposite to the quick-fix sugars found in foods like biscuits, which can contribute to highs and lows of energy and mood.

MAJOR NUTRIENTS PER MEDIUM-SIZED PEAR

KCalories	58
Total fat	Trace
Protein	0.68 g
Carbohydrate	27.52 g
Fibre	5.5 g
Vitamin C	7.5 mg
Potassium	212 mg

Pear, beetroot and spinach juice

SERVES 1   (A)(V)(Q)

1 beetroot, trimmed, peeled
   and chopped
1 pear, cored and chopped
25 g/1 oz fresh spinach leaves,
   plus one to decorate
filtered water, to taste

Method

1 Place the beetroot, pear and spinach in a food processor or blender and process. Dilute with filtered water to taste. Pour into a glass and decorate with the spinach leaf. Serve immediately.

18

PASSION FRUIT

The name may refer to religious rather than sexual passion, but the rich antioxidant status of this fruit nonetheless renders it potent as a fertility boost.

With its high levels of antioxidant vitamin C, vitamin A and beta carotene, including passion fruit in your diet can help protect you against the day-to-day damage caused by environmental factors that can harm sperm and eggs. Vitamin C is water-soluble and so protects watery areas of the body between and inside cells, as well as improving sperm count and quality. Vitamin A and beta carotene are fat-soluble, which means they protect the fat-rich testes and semen, and cell walls of the egg and womb. Antioxidants also stop the male immune system from destroying its own sperm, and the fibre in passion fruit sweeps harmful toxins out of the body via the digestive system.

- Vitamin C protects all cells from environmental harm and improves sperm count and quality.
- Vitamin A and beta carotene protect the testes, womb and egg from damage.
- All of the above antioxidants prevent the male immune system attacking its own sperm.
- High fibre removes toxins that increase the risk of infertility.

Practical tips:
Choose passion fruit that looks wrinkled because this means the fruit has ripened. Keep in the fridge for up to a week. The pulp and juice with seeds removed are most commonly used as flavouring, and are a healthy way to sweeten yogurts and top fruit salads.

DID YOU KNOW?

Its name and South American roots give passion fruit sexy connotations, and it is often served as an aphrodisiac in cocktail form. However, the alcoholic content of these drinks makes them difficult to recommend as a fertility treatment.

MAJOR NUTRIENTS PER MEDIUM-SIZED PASSION FRUIT

Kcalories	17
Total fat	0.13 g
Protein	0.4 g
Carbohydrate	4.21 g
Fibre	1.9 g
Vitamin C	5.4 mg
Vitamin A	229 IU
Beta carotene	134 mcg
Potassium	63 mg

Salmon with passion fruit salsa

SERVES 4 (**G**)(**A**)(**Q**)

4 salmon steaks, about 175 g/
   6 oz each
finely grated rind and juice of 1 lime
   or ½ lemon
pepper

Passion fruit salsa

1 large mango, peeled,
   stoned and diced
1 red onion, finely chopped
2 passion fruit
2 fresh basil sprigs
2 tbsp lime juice

Method

1 Rinse the salmon steaks under cold running water, pat dry with
   kitchen paper and place in a large, shallow, non-metallic dish.
   Sprinkle with the lime rind and pour the juice over them. Season
   to taste with pepper, cover and leave to stand while you make the
   passion fruit salsa.

2 Place the mango flesh in a bowl with the onion. Cut the passion fruit
   in half and scoop out the seeds and pulp with a teaspoon into the
   bowl. Tear the basil leaves and add them to the bowl with the lime
   juice then stir well. Cover with clingfilm and reserve until required.

3 Preheat the grill to high. Cook the salmon steaks under the grill for
   3–4 minutes on each side. Serve immediately with the salsa.

19

GREEN TEA

The antioxidant compound epigallocatechin gallate (EGCG) found in green tea is able to move inside cells and help protect our DNA from damage.

This is vital in terms of reproduction because our DNA determines the way in which we replicate cells. It is believed that the tea's active compounds, including EGCG, other similar catechins and hypoxanthine, may help the fertilization of oocytes, or egg cells, and create more embryos that are able to mature. Another bioflavonoid (plant chemical) in green tea is quercetin, which helps improve semen quality and aids circulation, bringing blood flow to the sexual organs. Prepare for pregnancy, and increase the chances of it, by switching from regular tea and coffee in advance so that you avoid caffeine withdrawal when pregnant.

- High in antioxidants, such as EGCG, that protect DNA from damage and enable cell replication.
- These compounds may also help fertilization of the egg to occur and embryos to grow.
- A healthy low-caffeine source that helps wean prospective mothers off tea and coffee in preparation for pregnancy.

Practical tips:
Green tea, which contains around 5 mg caffeine per cup, is made by drying the leaves of the tea plant *Camellia sinensis*. Black, 'normal', tea comes from the same plant but is fermented and much higher in caffeine, at around 50 mg a cup. Drink green tea in moderation when pregnant and don't leave to brew for more than a minute – this will ensure the caffeine content is low and the taste not too bitter.

DID YOU KNOW?
Some studies have suggested that drinking more than half a cup of green tea daily may actually double a woman's chances of conceiving, due to the tea's high antioxidant content.

MAJOR NUTRIENTS PER 225 ml/8 fl oz GREEN TEA

Kcalories – approx*	2
Total fat	0 g
Protein	0 g
Carbohydrate	0 g
Fibre	0 g
Catechins*	3.75 g

* can vary greatly between varieties and strength of brew

Spiced poached pears in green tea

SERVES 2 (A)(V)(Q)

2 slightly under-ripe pears,
   halved and peeled
1 tsp lemon juice
850 ml/1½ pints water
4 slices fresh ginger
2 star anise
1 cinnamon stick
1 tbsp clear honey
2 green tea bags

Method

1 Using a melon baller or teaspoon, scoop out the core of each pear. Squeeze the lemon juice over the pears to prevent them browning.

2 Bring the water to the boil in a large sauté pan. Reduce the heat to a simmer and add the ginger, star anise, cinnamon and honey. Stir until the honey melts then add the pears.

3 Simmer the pears for 15–20 minutes, partially covered, until tender, then remove from the pan using a slotted spoon. Increase the heat slightly, add the green tea and simmer for about 5 minutes until the cooking liquid has reduced and become syrupy.

4 Remove the spices and tea bags from the cooking syrup. Serve 2 pear halves per person with the syrup spooned over the top.

20 BRAZIL NUTS

Brazil nuts are excellent sources of selenium, zinc and vitamin E, which work together to produce good quality sperm and protect the egg from damage.

Brazil nuts are fantastic packages of protein, fibre, complex carbohydrates and healthy fatty acids. Each one of the nutritional elements they offer is needed for reproduction. Vitamin B6, zinc and magnesium contribute to the production of sex hormones, while healthy zinc and folate (folic acid) levels are essential for upcoming foetal development. Brazil nuts contain balanced levels of the minerals calcium and magnesium, too, which are excellent for bone growth; as 'calming minerals', they can also help reduce anxiety that can increase the risk of infertility.

- Contain high antioxidant levels, promoting healthy, intact sperm and egg.
- Each nut is nature's fertility package of fibre, fatty acids, carbohydrates, protein, vitamins and minerals.
- Vitamin B6, zinc and magnesium enable healthy sex hormone balance.
- Zinc and folate support the embryo as it matures.
- Contain balanced calcium and magnesium to support mother and baby bone health and reduce stress.

Practical tips:
Brazil nuts have a pleasant, creamy taste that makes them a perfect snack or protein addition to cereals, or fruit and yogurt. Like all nuts and seeds, their essential fatty acid content is easily damaged by heat and light so they should not be cooked.

DID YOU KNOW?

Organic Brazil nuts contain much higher amounts of selenium than non-organic nuts. You should also choose unshelled rather than shelled, for the same reason.

MAJOR NUTRIENTS PER 25 G/1 oz BRAZIL NUTS

Kcalories	197
Total fat	19.9 g
Omega-6 fatty acids	6,169 mg
Protein	4.3 g
Carbohydrate	3.7 g
Fibre	23 g
Vitamin B3	0.06 mg
Vitamin B6	0.30 mg
Vitamin E	1.72 mg
Folate	7 mcg
Calcium	48 mg
Magnesium	113 mg
Zinc	1.2 mg
Selenium	575 mcg

Oat and nut crunch mix

SERVES 8 (G) (A) (V) (Q)

olive oil, for brushing

90 g/3¼ oz jumbo oats

25 g/1 oz pine kernels

40 g/1½ oz pistachio nuts
  or hazelnuts

40 g/1½ oz almonds

40 g/1½ oz Brazil nuts, roughly
  chopped

2 tbsp sunflower seeds

2 tbsp pumpkin seeds

50 g/1¾ oz dried ready-to-eat
  apricots, chopped

40 g/1½ oz sultanas

1 tsp ground cinnamon

Method

1 Heat a non-stick frying pan over a medium heat and brush
  with a little oil. Add the oats and pine kernels and cook, stirring
  constantly, for 8–10 minutes, or until they smell nutty and look a
  little golden. Leave to cool.

2 Transfer the toasted oat mixture to a large bowl and add all the
  remaining ingredients then mix together well. Use as a topping for
  yogurt or fruit. It will keep for up to 2 weeks in the refrigerator.

First Trimester

Congratulations! You may be feeling changes to your body already. For many women, the first three months of pregnancy can be the hardest, with fatigue and morning sickness most likely to strike now. Being careful about what you eat can help, by ensuring steady blood-sugar levels, and providing the nutrients – such as B vitamins and iron – that may be depleted at this time. Folate (folic acid), vitamin E and zinc support the growth of the baby and placenta.

Certain foods can help minimize common symptoms, the best-known being ginger for nausea. Foods that support immunity are also particularly important now, when it is naturally lowered to protect the embryo from being rejected by the mother's body. Those foods that promote detoxification and the elimination of harmful substances also protect your baby at this delicate stage.

(G) Growth of baby

(B) Brain development of baby

(A) Immunity-supporting antioxidants

(N) Natural remedy

(V) Suitable for vegetarians

(Q) Quick and easy to prepare

21

GINGER

Ginger has been used for thousands of years as a medicine for nausea and morning sickness. Its active compound gingerol also encourages good digestion.

Being able to eat healthy, nutritious food is vital during all stages of pregnancy and this can be difficult in the early months when nausea is most likely. Ginger helps keep up the appetite by curbing nausea, and also helps rectify any digestive disharmony that may be contributing to the problem. It is a powerful antimicrobial, which means that it kills off harmful bacteria, yeasts and viruses that may harm the foetus. Its strong antioxidant action, derived from 12 different substances that together have a more protective effect than vitamin C, also protects the growing baby from damage.

- May help reduce morning sickness so that the expectant mother can retain her natural appetite; supports the absorption of vital nutrients.
- Contains high antioxidant levels that protect the embryo from damage.
- Kills off harmful bacteria and so helps prevent illness during this crucial time.

Practical tips:
A quick morning sickness remedy is ginger cordial with sparkling water. Others swear by ginger tea. It is available in tea bags, but a few slices of fresh ginger root with hot water is more potent. Ginger biscuits may be useful in emergencies, although the added sugar may exacerbate the problem in the long run.

DID YOU KNOW?

Studies have shown ginger to be superior to the common anti-nausea medicine Dramamine. It is especially useful during pregnancy, when a natural substance is preferable to a medication.

MAJOR NUTRIENTS PER 15 G/½ OZ FRESH GINGER

Kcalories	12
Total fat	0.11 g
Protein	0.27 g
Carbohydrate	2.66 g
Fibre	0.3 g
Vitamin C	2.4 mg
Potassium	62 mg

Gingered chicken and vegetable salad

SERVES 4 (A)(N)

4 spring onions, chopped

2.5-cm/1-inch piece fresh
   ginger, peeled and finely
   chopped

2 garlic cloves, crushed

3 tbsp vegetable oil

4 skinless, boneless chicken
   breasts, cut into 2.5-cm/
   1-inch cubes

Vegetable salad

1 tbsp vegetable oil

1 onion, sliced

2 garlic cloves, chopped

115 g/4 oz baby sweetcorn,
   halved

115 g/4 oz mangetout, halved
   lengthways

1 red pepper, deseeded
   and sliced

7.5-cm/3-inch piece
   cucumber, peeled,
   deseeded and sliced

4 tbsp soy sauce

1 tbsp honey

few Thai basil leaves

175 g/6 oz fine egg or
   buckwheat noodles

Method

1 Mix the spring onions, ginger, garlic and 2 tablespoons of the oil
   together in a shallow dish and add the chicken. Cover and marinate
   for at least 3 hours. Lift the meat out of the marinade and set aside.

2 Heat 1 tablespoon of the oil in a wok and stir-fry the onion for
   1–2 minutes. Add the garlic and the rest of the vegetables except
   the cucumber, and cook for 2–3 minutes until just tender. Add the
   cucumber, half the soy sauce, the honey and basil, and mix gently.

3 Soak the noodles for 2–3 minutes (check the packet instructions),
   or until tender, and drain well. Sprinkle the remaining soy sauce over
   them and arrange on plates. Top with the cooked vegetables.

4 Add the remaining oil to the wok, and stir-fry the chicken over a fairly
   high heat for 6 minutes, until cooked through and golden. Arrange
   the chicken on top of the salad and serve hot or warm.

22 ROOIBOS TEA

Rooibos is refreshing and caffeine-free. It provides antioxidants to support immunity, which is lowered in early pregnancy to prevent rejection of the embryo.

A mother's natural immune suppression in early pregnancy prevents the growing baby from being attacked as a foreign body. Rooibos is very high in polyphenols – protective antioxidants such as quercetin, rutin and ferulic acid – that support circulation and help prevent allergies that can heighten immune reactions. Rooibos also contains the antioxidant enzyme superoxide dismutase, which protects the body's cells – including a developing foetus – from damage by oxygen. Rooibos isn't technically a tea because it doesn't derive from the *Camellia sinensis* plant, but from a legume. This means that it is extremely low in the tannins present in 'normal' tea that can prevent the absorption of iron. Iron is vital in pregnancy because it supports blood flow to the growing baby.

- Rich antioxidant profile supports natural immunity, which becomes suppressed during pregnancy.
- These substances also support circulation and prevent allergies, so helping to prevent miscarriage.
- Low tannin content makes rooibos preferable to normal tea, as tannin in regular tea and coffee hinders iron absorption and can reduce blood flow to the baby.

Practical tips:
Drink with milk as 'normal' tea, or with lemon or honey. Limit intake to 2–3 cups a day in total. Some rooibos tea blends are mixed with herbal products that should be avoided during pregnancy.

DID YOU KNOW?
Rooibos tea has been used for hundreds of years by the African Bushman, one of the world's oldest peoples, especially to treat nausea, stomach cramps and constipation during pregnancy.

MAJOR NUTRIENTS PER 225 ML/8 FL OZ ROOIBOS TEA

Kcalories – approx*	2
Total fat	0 g
Protein	0 g
Carbohydrate	0 g
Fibre	0 g
Polyphenols*	60–80 mg

* can vary greatly between varieties and strength of brew

Spiced tea-soaked dried fruit salad

SERVES 4   Ⓐ Ⓝ Ⓥ

85 g/3 oz dried apricots
50 g/1¾ oz dried apple rings,
    chopped
50 g/1¾ oz dried pears
100 g/3½ oz sultanas
50 g/1¾ oz dried cherries
2 rooibos tea bags
several strips freshly pared lemon
    peel
1 cinnamon stick
1 star anise
Greek-style yogurt and honey,
    to serve

Method

1 Put the dried fruit and the tea bags in a heatproof bowl and pour over enough boiling water to cover the fruit by 2.5 cm/1 inch. Set aside and leave the fruit to stew in the water for at least 2 hours, but ideally overnight, stirring occasionally.

2 Tip the fruit and any remaining soaking liquid, the lemon peel, cinnamon stick and star anise into a saucepan over a medium heat. If necessary add extra water so the fruit is just covered and simmer for 10–20 minutes until the fruit is plump and soft.

3 Remove the pan from the heat and leave the fruit and liquid to cool.

4 Spoon the fruit into bowls, top with yogurt and honey and serve immediately.

23 AVOCADOS

The abundant oils and fibre in avocados help the liver to maintain healthy hormone levels. This supports the growing baby and helps prevent nausea.

Any fears about the fat content of avocados need to be discarded, especially during the first trimester of pregnancy. A growing baby needs these valuable oils to start developing, especially in fat-rich areas, such as the heart and brain. These oils carry with them fat-soluble nutrients such as vitamins A and E and the carotenoid lutein, which protect these delicate fatty areas from damage as they grow. The minerals calcium, magnesium and potassium – avocados contain 60 per cent more potassium than bananas – help support the mother's increasing metabolism and heart rate. They also help to regulate fluid balance and maintain healthy blood pressure. Although high blood pressure is less likely to pose a problem at this point of the pregnancy, support from the beginning as a preventative measure is advised.

MAJOR NUTRIENTS PER MEDIUM-SIZED AVOCADO

Kcalories	322
Total fat	29.47 g
Monounsaturated fat	19.7 g
Polyunsaturated fat	3.65 g
Protein	4.02 g
Carbohydrate	17.15 g
Fibre	13.5 g
Vitamin A	293 IU
Vitamin E	4.16 mg
Potassium	975 mg
Magnesium	58 mg
Calcium	24 mg
Lutein/Zeaxanthin	545 mcg

- Contain healthy fats that support liver health and the development of the baby's heart and brain.
- Fat-soluble nutrients, such as vitamins A and E and lutein, protect these fatty body parts from damage.
- Calcium, magnesium and potassium support the mother's increasing heart rate, metabolism and blood pressure.

Practical tips:
Avocado can be a pleasing snack even when morning sickness is an all-day problem, and it is a good choice if food intake is minimal. If solid food is off-putting, it can be made into a smoothie.

Avocado power pack

SERVES 1–2   (G) (B) (A) (V) (Q)

1 pear, peeled, cored and sliced

40 g/1½ oz baby leaf spinach

4 sprigs parsley

¼ cucumber

½ ripe avocado, stoned and peeled

½ tsp spirulina powder (available
    from healthfood shops)

1 Brazil nut, roughly chopped

Method

1 Put the pear, spinach, parsley, cucumber and avocado into a food
   processor or blender and blend until smooth, then pour into a glass.

2 Mix the spirulina powder with just enough water to make a
   thick liquid, then swirl into the juice. Sprinkle the Brazil nut over,
   then serve.

24

WALNUT OIL

Walnut oil provides a great balance of fatty acids during the first trimester, at a time when the baby's nervous system is undergoing intense development.

The omega-6 fatty acids in walnut oil help the body to maintain a healthy balance between sex hormones, which lowers the risk of miscarriage. Walnut oil also contains useful levels of omega-3 fatty acids, needed to support a baby's developing brain and spinal cord. These omega-3 fatty acids, along with omega-9 fatty acids (oleic acid), support the baby's heart development, too. During this crucial time, when a healthy immune system is vital to ward off infections, walnut oil also offers high levels of the antioxidant substances ellagic acid and phytosterols. These help the liver eliminate toxins that can pose a danger to your pregnancy by damaging cells and increasing the chances of inflammation and infection.

- Omega-6 fatty acids balance the sex hormones, while omega-3 fatty acids support brain development.
- Omega-3 and omega-9 fatty acids help create a healthy heart and keep problematic inflammation at bay.
- Ellagic acid and phytosterols fight against toxins and infections that can increase the risk of miscarriage.

Practical tips:
Store walnut oil in dark glass bottles: the fatty acids it contains can absorb hormone-disrupting chemicals from plastic. It should also be stored away from heat and light. Heating walnut oil can create damaging trans fats, so save it for salad dressings and smoothies. Choose cold-pressed varieties and avoid roasted or toasted oils.

DID YOU KNOW?
Walnut oil contains melatonin, a substance our brains use as a hormone to regulate sleep patterns, which can be affected from very early pregnancy. It also protects genetic material, including DNA, from damage.

MAJOR NUTRIENTS PER 15 ML/1 TBSP WALNUT OIL

Kcalories	120
Total fat	13.6 g
Monounsaturated fat	3.1 g
Omega-3 fatty acids	1404 mg
Omega-6 fatty acids	7141 mg
Omega-9 fatty acids	2997 mg
Vitamin E	0.1 mg
Phytosterols	23.8 mg

Roasted winter salad with walnut oil dressing

SERVES 2 Ⓑ Ⓐ Ⓥ

1 parsnip, cut into batons

350 g/12 oz butternut squash,
    peeled, seeded and cut into
    large bite-sized pieces

1 uncooked beetroot, halved and
    cut into wedges

1 large onion, cut into wedges

1 tbsp olive oil

2 large garlic cloves, unpeeled

Dressing

2 tbsp walnut oil

2 tsp cider vinegar

½ tsp clear honey

1 tsp wholegrain mustard

pepper

1 tsp warm water

Method

1 Preheat the oven to 200°C/400°F/Gas Mark 6. Toss the parsnip, squash, beetroot and onion in the olive oil and arrange in a single layer in a large roasting tin. Add the garlic and roast, turning once, for 30–35 minutes, until tender.

2 Meanwhile, to make the dressing, mix together the walnut oil, vinegar, honey, mustard and pepper with the water.

3 When the vegetables and garlic are ready, transfer the vegetables to a serving dish and squeeze the garlic on to a plate. Mash the garlic with the back of a fork then stir into the dressing. Pour the dressing over the vegetables and serve warm or at room temperature.

25 POMEGRANATE

Pomegranate juice has been found to contain around three times the protective dose of antioxidant polyphenols of either red wine or green tea.

The polyphenols in the fruit help to increase the circulation, keeping a growing baby supplied with vital blood and oxygen. This may reduce the negative effects on the brain that a baby born before 34 weeks risks because it is starved of a steady flow of blood and oxygen. It will also provide a healthy dose of vitamin C and folate (folic acid) to encourage all growth and development. Pomegranate juice has been found to help problems associated with high altitude in pregnant women, such as air travel, which may be part of an expectant mother's life during these early stages. High potassium helps this effect by aiding hydration.

- Rich polyphenols help blood and oxygen flow to the baby's brain and may reduce the risk of damage if born prematurely.
- Contains vitamin C and folate, which support all growth processes.
- Pomegranate juice has been shown to help reduce the negative effects of flying, while potassium assists hydration.

Practical tips:
Pomegranate juice has risen in popularity in the last few years and is now widely available. It is high in sugar, however, so limit consumption to a few glasses a day and dilute by up to half with water. It is even better to eat the fruit because you will also get the benefit of the cleansing fibre. Avoid pomegranate seed extract during pregnancy, because it can stimulate uterine contractions.

DID YOU KNOW?

Pomegranates were the primary symbol of Aphrodite, the Greek goddess of love who gave her name to 'aphrodisiac'. In Iran, these wonder fruits are recommended to pregnant women for their iron content.

MAJOR NUTRIENTS PER MEDIUM-SIZED POMEGRANATE

Kcalories	234
Total fat	3.3 g
Protein	4.71 g
Carbohydrate	52.73 g
Fibre	11.3 g
Vitamin C	28.8 mg
Folate	107 mcg
Calcium	28 mg
Magnesium	34 mg
Potassium	666 mg
Iron	0.85 mg
Selenium	1.4 mcg

Chicken with pomegranate salsa

SERVES 2 Ⓖ Ⓑ Ⓐ Ⓝ Ⓠ

2 x 175 g/6 oz skinless, boneless
    chicken breasts
1 tbsp olive oil
salad leaves, to serve
salt and pepper

Pomegranate salsa
1 small avocado
1 tbsp diced red onion
2.5-cm/1-inch piece cucumber,
    deseeded and diced
juice of ½ lime
2 tbsp chopped fresh coriander
4 heaped tbsp pomegranate seeds

Method

1 Flatten the chicken breasts with a meat mallet or the end of a rolling
   pin. Heat a griddle pan, brush the chicken with oil, season with salt
   and pepper, then griddle for about 6 minutes over a medium–high
   heat, turning once, until blackened in places and cooked through.

2 Halve the avocado, prise out the stone, then peel away the skin.
   Cut the avocado into small chunks and place in a bowl with the red
   onion, cucumber, lime juice, coriander and pomegranate. Season
   with pepper and stir gently until combined.

3 Serve the chicken with salad leaves and a spoonful of the salsa.

26

CELERY

Eating celery is one of the easiest ways to help bring down high blood pressure, which reduces the risk of later developing serious complications, including pre-eclampsia.

Celery contains two substances, apigenin and phthalide, that widen blood vessels, and three minerals, potassium, calcium and magnesium, that relax them. The combined effect is to keep blood pressure at a healthy level. Celery also contains the calming amino acid, tryptophan, from which we make the sleep and mood neurotransmitter serotonin, so it helps to minimize the stress and anxiety that can contribute to miscarriage risk. Its folate (folic acid) content helps prevent birth defects and the high potassium and water content help prevent dehydration and keep fluid available to the embryo. A mother-to-be can draw energy from the vitamin C, B vitamins and magnesium, making it less likely that she will turn to sugary snacks.

- Apigenin, phthalide, tryptophan, potassium, calcium and magnesium maintain healthy blood pressure and reduce stress.
- Contains folate for healthy foetal development.
- High potassium and water content ensures hydration of the mother and extra fluid for the embryo.
- Vitamin C, B vitamins and magnesium all balance blood sugar levels, promoting sustained energy.

Practical tips:
Celery is one of the simplest snacks – just munch on a stick or, for extra protein, dip some into hummus or a bean dip. It is an ideal bedtime nibble for people who find sleep difficult.

DID YOU KNOW?

Celery has a long history as a remedy for anxiety, high blood pressure and sleep problems, all of which can be experienced by women in pregnancy.

MAJOR NUTRIENTS PER 100 G/3½ OZ CELERY

Kcalories	16
Total fat	0.17 g
Protein	0.69 g
Carbohydrate	2.97 g
Fibre	1.6 g
Vitamin C	3.1 mg
Vitamin B3	0.32 mg
Vitamin B5	0.25 mg
Folate	36 mcg
Calcium	40 mg
Magnesium	11 mg
Potassium	260 mg

Gazpacho with celery salsa

SERVES 2   (G) (A) (N) (V)

2 x 45 g/1¾ oz slices day-old spelt
   bread, crusts removed
100 ml/3½ fl oz water, for soaking
500 g/1 lb 2 oz tomatoes,
   deseeded and skinned
1 small cucumber, peeled,
   deseeded and chopped
1 red pepper, deseeded and
   chopped
1 large red chilli, deseeded and
   finely chopped
1 large garlic clove
3 tbsp olive oil
juice of 1 lemon
pepper

Celery salsa

1 stick celery, sliced
1 small avocado, skinned, stoned
   and diced
6 large basil leaves

Method

1 Soak one of the slices of bread in the water for 5 minutes.

2 Put the bread, tomatoes and any juices, cucumber, red pepper,
   three-quarters of the chilli, the garlic, 1 tablespoon of the oil and the
   lemon juice (reserving 1 teaspoon) in a food processor or blender
   and process until combined but still a little chunky. Season with
   pepper then chill for 2–3 hours.

3 Just before serving, make the celery salsa. Put the celery, avocado,
   reserved lemon juice, basil and remaining chilli in a bowl, and stir
   until combined.

4 Cut the second slice of bread into cubes. Heat the remaining olive
   oil in a frying pan and fry the bread for about 5 minutes, or until
   golden and crisp.

5 Ladle the soup into bowls and top with a large spoonful of the salsa
   and the croûtons.

27

SUNFLOWER SEEDS

Sunflower seeds contain healthy doses of three key nutrients – folate, vitamin E and zinc. A developing baby needs each of these in order to develop and grow.

During the first 12 weeks, when the embryo is developing, nutrient-rich foods such as sunflower seeds support both the baby and the growing placenta. Vitamin E and folate (folic acid) help prepare the placenta's connection in the womb, ready for it to take over and sustain the pregnancy. They are also needed to develop the red blood cells that supply the placenta and baby with nutrients and oxygen, which they both need continually in order to flourish. The iron in sunflower seeds makes haemoglobin, the substance in blood that transports oxygen to where it is needed. Meanwhile vitamin E and magnesium keep the mother's muscles intact so that her body is able to support the growing baby and recover after birth. Selenium and zinc enable the body to create antioxidant enzymes that protect the baby from damage.

- Folate, vitamin E and zinc support growth of the baby and placenta.
- Vitamin E is needed to secure the placental link, and in combination with iron, safeguards the oxygen supply to the baby.
- Vitamin E and magnesium content maintains muscle health to support the baby and the mother post-pregnancy.
- Contain selenium and zinc to protect the embryo from toxins.

Practical tips:
Store in an airtight glass jar in a cupboard. The fatty acids are easily damaged, which can potentially be harmful, so avoid toasting. Sprinkle on salads, in cereals and on porridge.

DID YOU KNOW?

Increasing your protein intake during pregnancy can easily be achieved if you consume nuts and seeds such as sunflower seeds, as well as meat, fish, eggs, dairy, beans and whole grains.

MAJOR NUTRIENTS PER 15 G/½ OZ SUNFLOWER SEEDS

Kcalories	88
Total fat	7.72 g
Monounsaturated fat	2.78 g
Omega-6 fatty acids	3,457.2 mg
Omega-9 fatty acids	2,756.5 mg
Protein	3.12 g
Carbohydrate	3 g
Fibre	1.3 g
Vitamin E	5.28 mg
Folate	34 mcg
Magnesium	49 mg
Potassium	97 mg
Phosphorus	99 mg
Iron	0.79 mg
Selenium	7.9 mcg
Zinc	0.75 mg

Apricot, oat and sunflower seed bars

MAKES 12   (G)(B)(A)(V)

70 g/2½ oz jumbo oats
5 tbsp desiccated coconut
4 tbsp sunflower seeds
225 g/8 oz ready-to-eat dried
apricots, cut into small pieces
70 g/2½ oz raisins
100 ml/3½ fl oz fresh orange juice
30 g/1 oz flaked almonds

Method

1 Toast the oats in a dry frying pan for 5 minutes over a medium–low heat, tossing the pan regularly, until beginning to turn golden. Remove from the pan and leave to cool.

2 Put the coconut in the pan and toast, tossing the pan regularly, for 2 minutes, until light golden. Leave to cool.

3 Put the oats and sunflower seeds in a food processor or blender and process until coarsely chopped, then tip into a bowl.

4 Put the apricots, raisins and orange juice into the food processor or blender and process to a thick purée. Spoon the fruit purée into the bowl with the oat mixture. Add the toasted coconut and flaked almonds, and stir until combined into a thick paste.

5 Line a 25 x 18-cm/10 x 7-inch tin with rice paper or baking paper. Tip the fruit mixture into the tin and, using a palette knife, spread into an even layer about 1 cm/½ inch thick. Chill for about 1 hour in the refrigerator until firm, then slice into 12 pieces.

28 RASPBERRIES

Raspberries are a delicious way for a
mother-to-be to load up on antioxidants
that will protect the developing baby and
keep it supplied with vital oxygen.

Raspberries are one of the most abundant sources of antioxidants
in the plant kingdom. Their ample supply of vitamin C, quercetin
and proanthocyanidins helps prevent harmful free radicals (unstable
molecules) from damaging the susceptible new tissues of a
developing baby. These three also support the circulation so that
it can deliver oxygen and nutrients effectively. Vitamin C is water-
soluble, which means it keeps watery areas between and inside cells
free from harmful toxins, as well as the amniotic fluid that surrounds
and protects the baby. The high fibre of raspberries – at 20 per cent,
they have the highest fibre content of any fruit – takes a clean sweep
of the body, moving out what is unwanted. Another good reason
to include raspberries in the diet from early on is that they contain
fragine, a chemical thought to strengthen the uterus, which will stand
a mother in good stead when having birthing contractions later.

- Contain extremely high levels of antioxidants, which keep toxins from
  harming the baby, and help nourish it with oxygen and nutrients.
- High fibre content carries unwanted products out of the body.
- The substance fragine helps prepare the body for labour by
  strengthening the smooth muscle of the uterus.

Practical tips:
Raspberries are safe to eat at any time during pregnancy. A handful
of raspberries enjoyed daily as a snack or with cereal, yogurt or a
smoothie is a safe way to support constant detoxification.

DID YOU KNOW?
Raspberries are the richest
dietary source of ellagic
acid, which helps the liver
eliminate toxins and may also
alleviate morning sickness.

MAJOR NUTRIENTS PER 100 G/3½ OZ RASPBERRIES

Kcalories	52
Total fat	0.65 g
Protein	1.2 g
Carbohydrate	11.94 g
Fibre	6.5 g
Vitamin C	26.2 mg
Potassium	151 mg
Lutein	136 mcg

Raspberry and apple smoothie

SERVES 1 (A)(V)(Q)

1 eating apple, peeled, cored
   and chopped
2 tbsp chilled mineral water
55 g/2 oz fresh or thawed frozen
   raspberries
1 tsp clear honey (optional)
4 tbsp natural bio yogurt
ice cubes

Method

1 Put the apple in a food processor or blender with the mineral water
   and blend for 1 minute.

2 Reserve 2–3 raspberries for decoration and add the rest to the
   blender. Blend for 30 seconds before adding the honey, if using,
   and then add the yogurt. Blend for a further minute.

3 Place a few ice cubes in a glass, pour over the smoothie, decorate
   with the reserved raspberries and serve.

29

OATS

Oats provide a powerful combination of complex carbohydrates, ensuring a sustained release of energy at a time when the metabolic rate is increasing.

Oats and other slow-release foods balance your blood sugar by preventing sudden surges of sugar into the bloodstream. This keeps energy levels stable, helping to regulate appetite and prevent nausea, and keeps cravings for unhealthy foods at bay. The magnesium and zinc in oats also helps to keep blood sugar on an even keel, by supporting the production of insulin, as well as the hormones oestrogen and progesterone. At the same time, zinc, vitamin E, calcium, iron and folate (folic acid) work together to support the baby's growth and development. Oats also help to keep bowel movements regular; constipation is a common pregnancy symptom and needs addressing to ensure that the mother is able to eliminate harmful toxins and maintain a healthy hormone balance.

- Slow-release energy food that regulates blood sugar, preventing sugar cravings and helping to prevent morning sickness.
- Contain magnesium and zinc, needed to support the hormones that balance blood sugar and maintain pregnancy.
- Zinc, vitamin E, calcium, iron and folate are all necessary for foetal development.
- Help prevent constipation and remove toxins.

Practical tips:
Cooked oats in porridge are much easier to digest than the raw flakes found in muesli. Alternatively, soak the oats overnight in water or apple juice to increase their ability to relieve constipation.

DID YOU KNOW?

Oats contain beta glucans, chemicals that have positive effects on your immune system and which may therefore reduce the risk of early rejection of the growing embryo.

MAJOR NUTRIENTS PER 60 G/2¼ OZ OATS, UNCOOKED

Kcalories	233
Total fat	4 g
Protein	10 g
Carbohydrate	40 g
Fibre	6.4 g
Folate	34 mcg
Vitamin E	1.5 mg
Calcium	32 mg
Magnesium	106 mg
Potassium	257 mg
Zinc	2.4 mg
Iron	2.8 mg

Apple and spice porridge

SERVES 4   (G) (A) (N) (V) (Q)

600 ml/1 pint milk or water
115 g/4 oz medium rolled
*   porridge oats*
2 large apples, halved, cored
*   and grated*
½ tsp ground mixed spice
clear honey, to serve (optional)

Method

1 Put the milk in a saucepan and bring to the boil. Sprinkle in the oats, stirring constantly. Reduce the heat to low and leave the oats to simmer for 10 minutes, stirring occasionally.

2 When the porridge is creamy and much of the liquid has evaporated, stir in the grated apple and mixed spice. Spoon into bowls and drizzle with the honey, if using.

30 AUBERGINE

Aubergine provides a wide spread of the nutrients that work together to support a healthy pregnancy, including antioxidants that help protect a baby from toxic damage.

The chlorogenic acid found in aubergines is a powerful antioxidant. It also helps regulate blood sugar levels, promoting sustained energy levels, and assists our metabolism by reducing our body's uptake of sugar. Vitamins B3 and B5, zinc and manganese also help the body release the most energy possible from the food we eat, thereby reducing sugar cravings. Nasunin is another antioxidant in aubergine, which particularly protects fatty areas, such as the baby's growing heart, brain, liver and kidneys. Copper is a trace mineral needed for collagen production, the protein from which all human tissue is derived, and which is needed constantly to ensure the baby's continued development. The potassium in aubergine helps to keep blood pressure at a safe level.

- Chlorogenic acid protects the baby's cells from damage and regulates energy.
- Vitamins B3 and B5, zinc and manganese allow energy to be unlocked from food, ensuring a baby's growth.
- Nasunin prevents damage to fatty areas in the foetus.
- Contains copper, needed to make collagen for the baby to grow.
- Potassium ensures blood pressure stays within healthy parameters.

Practical tips:

It is recommended that everyone avoid salt beyond a little culinary seasoning whether pregnant or not, so rather than salt aubergines before cooking, try brushing slices with olive oil and grilling instead.

DID YOU KNOW?

Aubergine makes up part of the typical Mediterranean diet, which has been shown to have a positive effect on both the health of the mother and the child during pregnancy, resulting in a lower incidence of miscarriage and birth defects.

MAJOR NUTRIENTS PER 100 G/3½ OZ AUBERGINE

Kcalories	24
Total fat	0.19 g
Protein	1.01 g
Carbohydrate	5.7 g
Fibre	3.4 g
Vitamin B3	0.65 mg
Vitamin B5	0.28 mg
Zinc	0.16 mg
Copper	0.08 mg
Manganese	0.25 mg
Potassium	230 mg

Caponata

SERVES 2   (G) (B) (A) (V) (Q)

1 medium aubergine, cut into large,
   bite-sized pieces

3 tbsp olive oil

1 onion, chopped

3 garlic cloves, chopped

1 stick celery, thinly sliced

400 g/14 oz canned plum
   tomatoes

1 tsp red wine vinegar

½ tsp sugar

2 tbsp capers, drained and rinsed

4 fresh basil sprigs, leaves torn,
   to garnish

Method

1 Steam the aubergine for 10 minutes, until tender.

2 Meanwhile, heat the olive oil in a saucepan and sauté the onion for
   5 minutes, until softened. Add the garlic and celery and cook for
   another 5 minutes.

3 Add the tomatoes to the pan and break them down using the
   back of a spatula. Stir in the red wine vinegar, sugar, capers and
   aubergine, then bring to the boil. Reduce the heat and simmer,
   part-covered, for 10 minutes, until reduced and thickened.

4 Season with pepper then divide between two bowls and scatter
   over the basil to serve.

31

APPLES

Eating an apple can satisfy a sweet craving, helping to support changing demands on energy and a developing appetite, while sustaining blood sugar levels.

Regulating blood sugar levels to avoid highs and lows is the most fundamental way to control appetite, which can increase or decrease during the early stages of pregnancy. Keeping something in the stomach at all times can help keep nausea at bay and choosing an apple may stop an expectant mother from reaching for unhealthy foods such as biscuits and caffeine. It is high levels of the fibre pectin that makes the release of sugar in apples so slow. The pectin also holds onto toxins in the bowel so that they can be safely removed from the body and the baby. The antioxidant quercetin in apples supports immunity at a time when it is naturally low and encourages blood flow, taking oxygen and nutrients to the womb.

- Apples naturally regulate blood sugar levels to correct appetite, reduce cravings for caffeine and sugar and help prevent nausea.
- Pectin removes harmful toxins from the body.
- Quercetin's antioxidant action supports immunity and circulation.

Practical tips:
Non-organic apples are sprayed with more pesticides than other fruits, so choose organic to reduce the amount of toxins you take into your body. An apple a day is an easy way to keep your bowels regular, and you can also make apple purée with added plums, prunes or dried apricots if you need some extra help.

DID YOU KNOW?
Eating four or more apples a week during pregnancy may reduce the likelihood of childhood asthma in your baby. Studies have shown them to be the one common dietary factor in mothers whose children had the best airway development.

MAJOR NUTRIENTS PER MEDIUM-SIZED APPLE

Kcalories	95
Total fat	0.31 g
Protein	0.47 g
Carbohydrate	25.13 g
Fibre	4.4 g
Vitamin C	8.4 mg
Vitamin A	98 mg
Potassium	195 mg

Oaty apple and cinnamon muffins

MAKES 12 (A) (N) (V)

oil or melted butter, for greasing
    (if using)
200 g/7 oz wholemeal plain flour
75 g/2¾ oz fine oatmeal
2 tsp baking powder
70 g/2½ oz soft light brown sugar
1 tsp ground cinnamon
2 large eggs
225 ml/8 fl oz milk
100 ml/3½ fl oz groundnut oil
1 tsp vanilla extract
2 eating apples, cored and grated

Method

1 Preheat the oven to 180°C/350°F/Gas Mark 4. Grease a 12-cup muffin tin or line with 12 paper cases.

2 Sift together the flour, oatmeal and baking powder into a large bowl, adding any husks that remain. Stir in the sugar and cinnamon.

3 Lightly beat the eggs in a large bowl then beat in the milk and oil. Make a well in the centre of the dry ingredients and pour in the beaten liquid ingredients. Add the vanilla extract and stir gently until just combined; do not over-mix.

4 Stir the apple into the mixture. Spoon the mixture into the prepared muffin tin. Bake in the preheated oven for 25–30 minutes until risen, golden brown and firm to the touch.

5 Leave the muffins in the tin for 5 minutes, then serve warm or transfer to a wire rack and leave to cool.

32 MINT

Mint has a gently calming effect, making it useful in early pregnancy when anxiety is common, while its stomach-soothing properties can alleviate morning sickness.

Mint is known mainly for its ability to soothe and relax the smooth muscle and lining of the digestive tract, helping to reduce stomach pains, nausea and heartburn, commonly experienced by women in the first trimester of pregnancy. This helps to relieve stress in the abdomen and stomach that can result in tension in the rest of the body, even causing constipation and subsequent toxic accumulation. Cleverly, mint can destroy unwanted harmful bacteria before it enters the bloodstream and potentially affects the growing embryo, while at the same time supporting the digestive environment that enables good probiotic bacteria to flourish.

• May help calm the whole body, helping to relieve the anxiety that is common in early pregnancy.
• Soothes the stomach to help reduce nausea, indigestion, constipation and stomach pains.
• Helps prevent harmful bacteria reaching the baby.

Practical tips:
Mint is sometimes contraindicated in pregnancy as a herb that can bring on uterine contractions in women susceptible to miscarriage. However, this only applies to high doses, as you might get in supplements or herbal medicines. In normal culinary use, such as a few cups of mint tea per day, or the fresh leaf added to a smoothie, dressing or salad, mint is safe and beneficial.

DID YOU KNOW?

Using mint to relieve aches, pains and anxieties during pregnancy goes back millennia to the Ancient Greeks, who named it mintha after a mythological nymph who was turned into a plant by Persephone.

MAJOR NUTRIENTS PER 15 G/½ OZ MINT

Kcalories	7
Total fat	0 g
Protein	0.5 g
Carbohydrate	1.2 g
Fibre	1 g
Folate	16 mcg
Calcium	30 mg
Magnesium	9 mg
Potassium	69 mg
Iron	1.8 mg

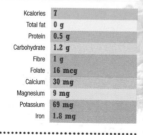

Mint and cannellini bean dip

SERVES 6 (G) (A) (N) (V) (Q)

175 g/6 oz canned cannellini
   beans, rinsed and drained
1 small garlic clove, crushed
1 bunch of spring onions,
   roughly chopped
handful fresh mint leaves
2 tbsp tahini
2 tbsp olive oil
1 tsp ground cumin
1 tsp ground coriander
lemon juice
pepper

Method

1 Put the cannellini beans into a bowl. Add the garlic, spring onions, mint, tahini and olive oil. Mash well until smooth. Stir in the cumin, coriander and lemon juice.

2 Season to taste with pepper. Mix thoroughly, cover with clingfilm and set aside in a cool place, but not the refrigerator, for 30 minutes, to allow the flavours to develop fully.

3 Spoon the dip into individual bowls and serve at room temperature.

33 LIVE YOGURT

Live yogurt retains the bacteria used to ferment the milk and has a long tradition of supporting immunity and reducing digestive problems.

The immune-supporting effects of live yogurt occur by increasing and protecting the probiotic beneficial bacteria that naturally colonizes our digestive tracts. This reduces inflammation and helps prevent intolerances and allergies. Yogurt also helps regulate digestion, reducing the incidence of diarrhoea and, particularly in pregnancy, constipation that may be at the heart of other symptoms, such as nausea, heartburn, flatulence and bloating. Any build-up of waste products in the intestines needs to be addressed at the start of pregnancy because it can lower the body's immunity and its ability to rid itself of toxins. Yogurt is a complete protein and a vegetarian source of vitamin B12, which means it is well equipped to support the baby's developing brain and body.

- Supports beneficial bacteria for immunity and detoxification.
- Ensures good digestive function, helping relieve nausea, heartburn, gas and bloating.
- Contains protein and vitamin B12, needed to form the baby's brain and body tissues.

Practical tips:
Live Greek-style yogurt can be easier to digest because it contains less lactose and more protein, and may help women with morning sickness feel fuller easily. Choose organic dairy products if possible, to reduce your exposure to hormones and antibiotics.

DID YOU KNOW?

Yogurt isn't only for eating, but can also help to relieve vaginal thrush symptoms when used topically. Thrush is a common pregnancy complaint and a warning to cut down on sugar in the diet.

MAJOR NUTRIENTS PER 100 ML/3½ FL OZ NATURAL YOGURT, FULL-FAT

Kcalories	61
Total fat	3.25 g
Protein	3.47 g
Carbohydrate	4.66 g
Vitamin A	99 IU
Vitamin B2	0.14 mg
Vitamin B5	0.39 mg
Vitamin B12	0.37 mcg
Choline	15.2 mg
Calcium	121 mg
Potassium	155 mg

Apricot and yogurt cups

SERVES 4–6   (G) (B) (A) (N) (V) (Q)

600 ml/1 pint natural bio yogurt

few drops of almond extract

2–3 tsp clear honey, warmed

55 g/2 oz whole blanched almonds,
   thinly sliced

175 g/6 oz ready-to-eat dried
   apricots, cut into small pieces

Method

1 Line a 12-cup bun tin with small paper cake cases.

2 Spoon the yogurt into a mixing bowl, add the almond extract,
   honey, almonds and apricots and stir well.

3 Spoon the mixture into the paper cases and freeze for
   1½–2 hours, or until just frozen. Serve immediately.

34 BLACK BEANS

All beans have antioxidant properties but black beans are particularly special. The purple proanthocyanidins they contain ensure good blood flow to the womb.

The antioxidant power of black beans is around ten times that of the equivalent weight of oranges, so a meal based on these will help keep a baby safe by supporting the mother's immunity. Black beans also supply a great dose of folate (folic acid), not only needed for the baby's neural tube to form in the first four weeks of pregnancy, but later on for the production of the entire nervous system, producing red blood cells and all new cell growth. Vitamin B1 aids these processes by helping the body produce the energy needed to make it all happen. The high levels of protein, calcium, magnesium and potassium in black beans also help strengthen the mother's muscles as they prepare to accommodate the growing baby.

- High antioxidant levels protect the growing baby from harm and help safeguard the pregnancy.
- Folate and vitamin B1 play crucial roles as the baby's nervous system grows and the mother's blood volume increases.
- Protein, calcium, magnesium and potassium prepare the stomach muscles to stretch and support the baby.

Practical tips:
There is little nutritional difference between dried or canned beans. Look for those that do not contain salt or additives. If cooking from dried, pre-soaking helps break down the fibres that can cause flatulence. Soak overnight or boil for two minutes and then allow the beans to stand, covered in the water, for two hours.

DID YOU KNOW?

Nature provides combinations of nutrients that help regulate the body. The minerals in beans, for example, naturally maintain good blood pressure levels, which can be jeopardised in early pregnancy as blood volume begins to increase.

MAJOR NUTRIENTS PER 100 G/3½ OZ DRIED BLACK BEANS

Kcalories	341
Total fat	1.42 g
Protein	21.6 g
Carbohydrate	62.36 g
Fibre	15.2 g
Vitamin B1	0.9 mg
Folate	444 mcg
Vitamin E	0.21 mg
Calcium	123 mg
Magnesium	171 mg
Potassium	1,483 mg
Zinc	3.65 mg

Mixed bean chilli

SERVES 4–6 Ⓖ Ⓑ Ⓐ Ⓥ Ⓠ

2 tbsp olive oil

1 onion, chopped

2 garlic cloves, finely chopped

1 fresh red chilli, deseeded
   and chopped

1 small red pepper, deseeded
   and chopped

1 tsp ground cumin

1 tsp ground coriander

1 tsp dried thyme

2 tomatoes, deseeded
   and chopped

115 g/4 oz dried red kidney beans,
   soaked overnight, drained
   and rinsed

115 g/4 oz dried black beans,
   soaked overnight, drained
   and rinsed

115 g/4 oz dried pinto beans,
   soaked overnight, drained
   and rinsed

150 ml/5 fl oz vegetable stock

pepper

chopped fresh coriander, to garnish

Method

1 Heat the oil in a large, heavy-based saucepan. Add the onion
   and cook over a medium heat, stirring occasionally, for 5 minutes.
   Stir in the garlic, chilli and red pepper and cook for another
   3 minutes. Add the cumin, coriander and thyme and cook, stirring,
   for 1–2 minutes.

2 Add the tomatoes, drained beans and stock and bring to the boil
   then reduce the heat and simmer, part-covered, for 12 minutes,
   stirring occasionally.

3 Season with pepper, then ladle half into a bowl. Mash well with a
   potato masher then return the mashed beans to the pan. Serve
   immediately, sprinkled with chopped fresh coriander.

35 ALMONDS

Almonds contain high levels of vitamin E, which protects the baby's delicate fat cells and helps produce both mother and baby's increasing red blood cell numbers.

MAJOR NUTRIENTS PER 25 G/1 oz ALMONDS

Kcalories	174
Total fat	15 g
Monounsaturated fat	9.27 g
Omega-6 fatty acids	3,619 mg
Omega-9 fatty acids	9,182 mg
Protein	6.6 g
Carbohydrate	6 g
Fibre	3 g
Vitamin B3	1.01 mg
Vitamin B5	0.14 mg
Vitamin E	7.4 mg
Calcium	80 mg
Magnesium	80 mg
Potassium	211.5 mg
Phosphorus	145.2 mg
Zinc	1.51 mg
Phytosterols	42.9 mg

The omega-6 fatty acids, B vitamins, zinc and magnesium in almonds not only help to regulate oestrogen and progesterone, which is essential to maintain pregnancy and reduce the risk of miscarriage, but also help keep up the mother's energy, good mood and positive outlook. The minerals calcium and magnesium are also present, in a perfectly balanced ratio, helping to soothe muscle tension, maintain healthy blood pressure and keep the mother's brain firing on all cylinders. In the first trimester, the baby is busy storing calcium ready to build bone and is taking this from its mother. If there is not enough calcium in the diet, the mother's personal stores will be the ones to suffer, often resulting in tooth decay or increased risk of osteoporosis later in life.

- Vitamin E helps prevent inflammation and ensure immunity, protect fatty areas of the baby's body and create red blood cells.
- Omega-6 fatty acids, B vitamins, zinc and magnesium regulate hormones, energy and mood.
- Contain calcium and magnesium for healthy blood pressure, baby's bone growth and topping up the mother's stores.

Practical tips:
As an easy, portable snack, almonds help prevent drops in blood sugar that can cause nausea, fatigue and dizziness. For some women, snacking every four hours is the only way to reduce these symptoms. Eat them raw and store away from heat and light.

Savoury almond nut butter

SERVES 10   (G) (A) (V) (Q)

150 g/5½ oz blanched
  whole almonds
5 tbsp light olive oil
2 tsp fajita spice blend
pinch of sea salt

Method

1 Put the almonds and oil in a food processor or blender and process to a coarse paste.
2 Transfer the nut butter to a bowl, then stir in the spice blend and salt. Cover and store in the refrigerator.

36 CHICKEN

Chicken is a dense source of protein that will provide the building blocks for a baby's development and growth. Protein forms the basis of every part of the human body.

We also receive a good dose of iron when eating chicken. The iron in chicken, and other animal products, is the most easily absorbed by the body. We are then able to use it to make haemoglobin to transport oxygen and create energy. Fatigue in the first trimester can often signal low iron stores and should be discussed with a doctor. It is low levels of iron and its helpmate vitamin B6, also present in chicken, that most often contribute to morning sickness. As well as helping our utilization of iron, B6 regulates the hormone oestrogen, which can contribute to nausea and even vomiting at this early stage when the hormone is peaking. The selenium in chicken helps eliminate toxic metals, such as mercury and lead, which can harm the foetus.

- Dense protein that provides the building materials a baby needs for full development.
- Contains easily utilized iron with vitamin B6, helping the body to create energy and combat fatigue and morning sickness.
- Selenium helps detoxify toxic metals that are harmful to the foetus.

Practical tips:
A free-range chicken will have a higher protein-to-fat ratio than other birds because it has been active, and is more likely to have been fed more nutritious food. Organic is the best option during pregnancy, because the hormones and antibiotics present in non-organic meat may interfere with a mother's own hormones and immunity.

DID YOU KNOW?

You may have seen hyaluronic acid in the ingredients lists of skin care creams, as it plumps out the skin. It is naturally present in chicken and will help a growing baby to hold onto water, keeping it fully hydrated.

MAJOR NUTRIENTS PER 100 G/3½ OZ CHICKEN, SKIN REMOVED

Kcalories	114
Total fat	2.59 g
Saturated fat	0.57 g
Monounsaturated fat	0.76 g
Protein	21.23 g
Carbohydrate	0 g
Vitamin B3	10.43 mg
Vitamin B5	1.43 mg
Vitamin B6	0.75 mg
Selenium	32 mcg
Iron	0.37 mg

Chicken and barley stew

SERVES 4   (G) (B) (A)

2 tbsp olive oil

8 small, skinless chicken thighs

500 ml/18 fl oz chicken stock

100 g/3½ oz pearl barley, rinsed
    and drained

200 g/7 oz small new potatoes,
    scrubbed and halved
    lengthways

2 large carrots, peeled and sliced

1 leek, trimmed and sliced

2 shallots, sliced

1 tbsp tomato purée

1 bay leaf

1 courgette, trimmed and sliced

2 tbsp chopped fresh flat-leaf
    parsley, plus extra sprigs
    to garnish

2 tbsp cornflour

4 tbsp water

salt and pepper

Method

1   Heat the oil in a large saucepan over a medium heat. Add the
    chicken and cook for 3 minutes, then turn over and cook for a
    further 2 minutes. Add the stock, barley, potatoes, carrots, leek,
    shallots, tomato purée and bay leaf. Bring to the boil, lower the heat
    and simmer for 30 minutes.

2   Add the courgette and chopped parsley, cover the pan and cook
    for a further 20 minutes, or until the chicken is cooked through.
    Remove the bay leaf and discard.

3   In a separate bowl, mix the cornflour with the water and stir into a
    smooth paste. Add to the stew and cook, stirring, over a low heat
    for a further 5 minutes. Season to taste with a little salt and pepper.

4   Remove from the heat, ladle into warmed serving bowls and garnish
    with sprigs of fresh parsley.

37 POLLOCK

As a white fish, pollock's protein levels are comparative to chicken, but this fish also offers DHA, the omega-3 fatty acid responsible for brain development in babies.

Oily fish is the best source of omega-3 fatty acids, but lower levels can also be found in pollock (about 20–25 per cent of the amount in salmon and mackerel). Omega-3 DHA (docosahexaenoic acid) is necessary for the development of the central nervous system, eyes and brain. A woman's daily DHA requirements are at least 200 mg and increase during pregnancy. Some studies have found a link between DHA intake in pregnancy and a baby's future cognitive development, though the evidence is not conclusive. Brain development is also supported by choline, a B vitamin present in pollock. Vitamin A – crucial in the first stage of pregnancy for the development of the heart, lungs, kidneys, eyes, bones, lungs, brain and nervous system – is in safe levels in pollock. The fish is also a source of another antioxidant, selenium, which helps to protect the baby's growing organs and to support your immune system.

- Contains protein and DHA to support foetal brain and nervous system development.
- Choline is needed for brain development.
- Contains a safe amount of vitamin A, as well as selenium, to help protect your baby and support your own immune system.

Practical tips:
Pollock has a less pungent taste and smell than oily fish, and this can be helpful for women who are put off the thought of fish during early pregnancy. Oilier fish can be reintroduced later in pregnancy.

DID YOU KNOW?
Pollock is low in the toxic metal mercury, which is known to contaminate tuna and swordfish and is especially harmful for pregnant women, increasing the risk of premature birth.

MAJOR NUTRIENTS PER 100 G/3½ oz FRESH POLLOCK

Kcalories	92
Total fat	8.8 g
Omega-3 fatty acids	443 mg
Protein	83 g
Carbohydrate	0.2 g
Vitamin A	37 IU
Vitamin E	0.4 IU
Vitamin B3	3.3 mg
Vitamin B5	0.4 mg
Vitamin B6	0.3 mg
Vitamin B12	3.2 mcg
Folate	24 mcg
Choline	65 mg
Selenium	36.5 mcg

Pollock with watercress sauce

SERVES 4   (G) (B) (Q)

*4 pollock or other white
   fish fillets, each about
   175 g/6 oz, skinned*
juice of ½ lemon
5 tbsp olive oil
1 shallot, finely chopped
1 garlic clove, finely chopped
*115 g/4 oz watercress, finely
   chopped*
250 ml/9 fl oz crème fraîche
salt and pepper
watercress sprigs, to garnish
new potatoes, to serve

Method

1 Sprinkle the fish fillets with the lemon juice and season with pepper.
Heat 3 tablespoons of the olive oil in a frying pan. Add the fish and
cook over a medium–low heat for 3–4 minutes on each side.

2 Meanwhile, heat the remaining oil in a saucepan. Add the shallot
and garlic and cook over a low heat, stirring occasionally, for
5 minutes, until soft. Stir in the watercress and cook, stirring
occasionally, for 2 minutes, until wilted. Stir in the crème fraîche,
season to taste with a little salt and pepper and heat gently.

3 Using a fish slice, transfer the fish fillets to warmed serving plates.
Spoon the sauce over them, garnish with watercress sprigs and
serve immediately with new potatoes.

38 OLIVE OIL

The fat profile of olive oil is similar to human breast milk. As such, it can help to support a baby's growth throughout pregnancy, and beyond if the baby is breastfed.

As one of the staples of the Mediterranean diet, olive oil is the oil to choose if you want to pass on the immune-enhancing properties of that diet – derived from substances including quercetin and oleic acid – to a developing child. The vitamin E in olive oil has been shown to be a supportive factor in the development of a baby's liver, kidneys and pancreas, important if a baby is born prematurely. Thanks to the compound oleocanthal, which has the same anti-inflammatory action as ibuprofen, olive oil also helps to relieve those pregnancy aches and pains, completely naturally.

- Contains healthy fats and immune-supporting chemicals that can be passed on to a child even beyond pregnancy.
- Consumption during pregnancy has been shown to produce better breathing patterns in babies.
- Vitamin E helps reduce the risk of problems in the liver, kidneys and pancreas in premature infants.
- Oleocanthal acts as a potent anti-inflammatory, so reducing aches and pains.

Practical tips:
Choose the best quality extra-virgin, cold-pressed olive oil that you can afford and use it for salad dressings. Its high monounsaturated fat content means that it can be safely used when cooking at medium temperatures, such as when stir-frying or roasting.

DID YOU KNOW?

Olive oil is a fabulous natural moisturizer during early pregnancy. It will help prevent stretch marks later, and is free of the hormone-disrupting chemicals found in many commercial toiletries.

MAJOR NUTRIENTS PER 15 ml/1 tbsp OLIVE OIL

Kcalories	132
Total fat	15 g
Monounsaturated fat	4.62 g
Omega-6 fatty acids	1,464 mg
Omega-9 fatty acids	10,689 mg
Carbohydrate	0 g
Vitamin E	2.15 mg

Green pesto sauce

MAKES 125 ML /4 FL OZ   (G) (A) (N) (Q)

40 fresh basil leaves
3 garlic cloves, crushed
25 g/1 oz pine nuts
50 g/1¾ oz Parmesan cheese,
   grated finely
2–3 tbsp extra virgin olive oil
pepper

Method

1 Rinse the basil leaves and pat them dry with kitchen paper. Put the basil leaves, garlic, pine nuts and Parmesan into a food processor or blender and blend for 30 seconds or until smooth. Alternatively, pound all of the ingredients in a mortar with a pestle.

2 If you are using a food processor or blender, keep the motor running and slowly add the olive oil. Alternatively, add the oil drop by drop while stirring briskly. Season with pepper, to taste.

39

PAPAYA

Papaya contains a digestive enzyme, papain, which breaks down the proteins we eat, helping to reduce pregnancy heartburn, constipation and nausea.

The hormone progesterone steadily rises in a mother's body during pregnancy, softening the muscles to allow the womb to expand. It can have the adverse effect of softening digestive muscles, resulting in heartburn, nausea and constipation. The papain in papaya may help to correct this. The vitamin C in this fruit aids iron and calcium absorption. Vitamin C supports thyroid function, too, so promoting the development of a baby's brain and nervous system, and the production of collagen for structural growth. The carotenoids beta carotene, lutein and zeanxathin in papaya protect the embryonic fatty areas, such as the heart, brain, eyes and skin, as they develop. Our bodies convert beta carotene to vitamin A as it is required, helping us to avoid a harmful overload of this vitamin.

- Contains papain, which helps the body digest protein, reducing morning sickness, sluggish digestion and heartburn.
- Vitamin C enables iron and calcium absorption, and supports thyroid function for brain development and collagen synthesis for skin, bone and organs.
- Carotenoids protect the baby's growing fatty areas and produce vitamin A as it is needed for a healthy heart, brain, eyes and skin.

Practical tips:

Include papaya in salads with fish or meat to break down these dense proteins. Do not take supplements while pregnant and avoid unripened papaya because it may cause uterine contractions.

DID YOU KNOW?

The rich colours of tropical fruit display their high carotenoid content. These antioxidants protect the fruit from UV damage from the sun as they ripen, just as they protect a growing baby's delicate body.

MAJOR NUTRIENTS PER MEDIUM-SIZED PAPAYA

Kcalories	120
Total fat	0.4 g
Protein	1.5 g
Carbohydrate	30 g
Fibre	5.5 g
Vitamin C	180 mg
Potassium	780 mg
Lutein/Zeanxathin	228 mcg
Beta carotene	839 mcg

Papaya, avocado and red pepper salad

SERVES 4–6   (G) (B) (A) (N) (V) (Q)

200 g/7 oz mixed salad leaves

2–3 spring onions, chopped

3–4 tbsp chopped fresh coriander

1 small ripe papaya

2 red peppers, deseeded, halved
   and thinly sliced

1 avocado

1 tbsp lime juice

3–4 tbsp pumpkin seeds (optional)

Dressing

juice of 1 lime

large pinch of paprika

large pinch of ground cumin

1 garlic clove, finely chopped

4 tbsp extra virgin olive oil

Method

1   Combine the salad leaves with the spring onions and coriander in a bowl. Mix well, then transfer the salad to a large serving dish.

2   Cut the papaya in half and scoop out the seeds with a spoon. Cut into quarters, remove the peel and slice the flesh. Arrange on top of the salad leaves. Add the peppers to the salad leaves. Cut the avocado in half around the stone. Twist apart, then remove the stone with a knife. Carefully peel off the skin, dice the flesh and toss in lime juice to prevent discoloration. Add to the other salad ingredients.

3   To make the dressing, whisk the lime juice, paprika, cumin, garlic and oil together in a small bowl. Pour the dressing over the salad and toss lightly. Sprinkle with pumpkin seeds, if using.

40 ROCKET

Rocket is a brassica and as such contains sulphoraphanes, chemicals that provide the optimum natural protection for a mother-to-be and a developing baby.

Sulphoraphanes neutralize toxins and enable you to produce antioxidant enzymes in the liver that work over and over again long after eating. This far-reaching effect can prevent damage to both the baby's DNA and body parts in support of full and healthy development. It can also stimulate the other antioxidants you receive in your diet, thereby increasing their protective power. Rocket has dark leaves because it contains high levels of carotenoid antioxidants, and these together with the high vitamin C, E and folate (folic acid) content support the growth of tissues in the baby's developing body. The calcium in rocket is the main mineral for bone growth, ably assisted by vitamin C and beta carotene. Meanwhile, potassium helps regulate body fluids to reduce puffiness and the risk of high blood pressure in pregnancy.

- Sulphoraphanes provide long-term natural antioxidant protection and rejuvenate other antioxidants so that they work at full power.
- Vitamins C and E and folate play interlinked roles in a baby's development.
- Contains calcium, vitamin C and beta carotene, which are all needed for skeleton building.
- Potassium helps prevent fluid retention and high blood pressure.

Practical tips:
Peppery rocket leaves stimulate digestion, making them a healthy basis for any salad. Add to Italian dishes at the end of cooking.

DID YOU KNOW?

Although full detoxification regimes are not advised during pregnancy because the released toxins could harm the baby, eating green leaves such as rocket naturally cleans out toxins on a safe, everyday basis.

MAJOR NUTRIENTS PER 15 G/½ OZ ROCKET

Kcalories	4
Total fat	0 g
Protein	0.4 g
Carbohydrate	0.5 g
Fibre	0.2 g
Vitamin C	2.3 mg
Folate	15 mcg
Vitamin E	1.5 mg
Calcium	24 mg
Potassium	55 mg
Beta carotene	214 mcg
Lutein/Zeaxanthin	533 mcg

Grilled prawns with rocket and radicchio

SERVES 4   (G) (A) (Q)

1 garlic clove, crushed

juice of ½ lemon

4 tbsp extra virgin olive oil

¼ tsp dried chilli flakes

250 g/9 oz large, raw, shelled
    prawns, without heads

8 radicchio leaves, sliced
    into ribbons

4 handfuls rocket

1 tsp balsamic vinegar

pepper

2 tbsp shredded fresh basil,
    to garnish

Method

1 Whisk the garlic and lemon juice with 3 tablespoons of the oil, chilli flakes, and pepper, to taste. Pour over the prawns and leave to marinate for 30 minutes.

2 Put the radicchio and rocket in a bowl. Toss with the remaining tablespoon of oil. Sprinkle with the vinegar and toss again. Divide the leaves between individual plates.

3 Preheat a ridged, cast-iron, griddle pan over a high heat. Add the prawns and grill for 2 minutes, turning and brushing with the marinade, until uniformly pink and cooked through. Arrange on top of the salad leaves and sprinkle with the basil.

3

Second Trimester

Now you are in the foetal stage, which is the most rapid period of growth until birth, and you really begin to see your baby growing. The placenta now works to supply the foetus with nutrients and oxygen, leaving you less tired and nauseous, but your heartbeat and blood volume are both raised, making it important that you keep up your supplies of iron, magnesium and vitamin B12. You need to provide quality nutrition to support your body and your baby's rapid growth and development.

As the hormone progesterone keeps rising to maintain your pregnancy, it may cause symptoms such as constipation and heartburn. Increased blood flow can lead to nosebleeds, easy bruising, haemorrhoids and varicose veins. Nutrition can help to prevent these or lessen their severity by encouraging good digestive and circulatory function.

(G) Growth of baby
(B) Brain development of baby
(A) Immunity-supporting antioxidants
(N) Natural remedy
(V) Suitable for vegetarians
(Q) Quick and easy to prepare

41

CAMOMILE

The mild sedatory effect of camomile tea can be a welcome relief at this stage, when thoughts about the developing pregnancy may interfere with sleep.

A growing bump can start to cause pelvic and back pain, and this together with breast tenderness makes some sleep positions uncomfortable. The chemicals apigenin and glycine in camomile soothe the body, making it easier to cope with discomfort and achieve a better quality of sleep. Camomile also has a refreshing effect, which has been known to help alleviate any nausea that may continue into the second trimester. Heartburn and constipation may be relieved by camomile because it helps to calm the nervous system, thus decreasing the stress that can contribute to these symptoms. The hippuric acid in camomile may also help prevent urinary tract infections (UTIs), which can result from the increasing pressure on the bladder and kidneys.

- Contains soothing apigenin and glycine, which help alleviate sleep problems.
- Camomile is a natural laxative and may ease digestive upsets.
- Hippuric acid helps keep UTIs such as cystitis at bay, which become more of a risk as blood flow increases.

Practical tips:
Don't drink herbal teas in large quantities during pregnancy because the effects of higher doses on the uterine muscle are still unclear. Place cold, used camomile tea bags on the eyes to relieve puffiness caused by insomnia or fluid retention. Avoid camomile if you are allergic to ragweed.

DID YOU KNOW?

Camomile tea is a popular sleep-aid during pregnancy, but you only need one or two cups. Any more can have an opposite, stimulating effect, which is increased if you add sugar.

MAJOR NUTRIENTS PER 225 ML/8 FL OZ CAMOMILE TEA

Kcalories – approx*	2
Total fat	0 g
Protein	0 g
Fibre	0 g
Carbohydrate	0.47 g

* can vary greatly between varieties and strength of brew

Camomile infusion

SERVES 2 Ⓝ Ⓥ Ⓠ

*2 tbsp camomile flowers or two
camomile tea bags*
40 g/1½ oz fresh ginger, sliced
600 ml/1 pint just-boiled water
1–2 tsp clear honey (optional)
*Ice cubes and lemon slices, to
serve (optional)*

Method

1 If making the infusion in a teapot*, warm the pot first, then add the camomile flowers or bags and the ginger. Allow the boiled water to cool for a minute then pour it into the teapot. Stir and leave to brew for 3–5 minutes.

2 Strain and pour the infusion into two cups, adding honey to taste, if using. The tea can also be served as a refreshing cold drink with ice cubes and a slice of lemon.

* Alternatively, place 1 tablespoon of camomile flowers, or 1 bag, directly into each cup. Divide the ginger between the cups, then pour over the boiling water. Leave the infusion to steep for 5 minutes, then strain, if preferred. Add honey, if using.

42

BEEF

Eating beef occasionally will ensure the body is well equipped to regulate increasing hormone levels because it is high in B vitamins and minerals.

During pregnancy, the body needs to make extra red blood cells, and the iron and vitamin B12 in beef enable this process. Meanwhile, the coenzyme Q-10 in beef helps create the necessary energy and supports the baby's heartbeat. Its B-vitamin profile facilitates protein metabolism, so that the mother can access the quality protein provided by the meat and use all these essential amino acids to build the baby's body. The zinc and selenium in beef also help the baby's tissues to grow, and keep the mother's own skin clear at a time when acne may be a problem due to increasing oestrogen levels.

- B vitamins and minerals regulate hormones, provide energy and support both mother and baby physically and mentally.
- Contains iron and vitamin B12 to support the increasing need for new red blood cells.
- Coenzyme Q-10 generates energy in the cells, especially the growing foetal heart.
- A source of quality protein, made accessible by the B vitamins that are also in the meat, promoting baby's growth and development.
- Zinc and selenium help keep the complexion clear.

Practical tips:
You don't need to eat beef often to enjoy the benefits, so buy good, lean cuts, preferably from grass-fed, organic sources. Non-organic meats contain potentially harmful hormones and antibiotics.

DID YOU KNOW?

As the need for energy increases, a dense protein such as beef can stop cravings for sugar. Instant energy sources in the form of cakes and biscuits may be tempting, but they offer a baby little nutritional value.

MAJOR NUTRIENTS PER 100 G/3½ OZ GROUND BEEF

Kcalories	215
Total fat	15 g
Saturated fat	5.87 g
Monounsaturated fat	6.56 g
Protein	18.59 g
Carbohydrate	0 g
Fibre	0 g
Vitamin B3	4.65 mg
Vitamin B5	0.55 mg
Vitamin B6	0.35 mg
Vitamin B12	2.17 mcg
Iron	2.09 mg
Zinc	4.48 mg
Selenium	15.8 mcg

Sizzling lemon grass beef with asparagus

SERVES 4　Ⓖ Ⓑ Ⓠ

15 spears asparagus, trimmed and
　sliced diagonally
2 tbsp vegetable oil
1 stalk lemon grass, peeled and
　finely chopped
200 g/7 oz beansprouts
1 red pepper, thinly sliced
1 tbsp chopped garlic
450 g/1 lb fillet steak, thinly sliced
5 tbsp chicken stock
juice and finely sliced zest of 1 lime
pepper

Method

1　Bring a saucepan of water to the boil and quickly blanch the
asparagus. Plunge into iced water.

2　Heat a wok over a high heat and add the oil. Add the lemon grass,
beansprouts, red pepper, garlic and beef and stir-fry for 1 minute.
Add the stock, asparagus and pepper to season, then stir-fry until
the beef is done. Add the lime juice and zest, stir for another
minute and remove from the heat. Serve immediately.

43 DRIED FIGS

Dried figs provide a healthy energy source and have a better mineral profile than most other fruit and vegetables, closely resembling that of human breast milk.

As the pregnant body expands, it is important to keep up potassium levels in order to maintain the right mineral balance across the body's increasing fluids. This is especially true if sickness in the first trimester led to vomiting, because this depletes potassium and the other electrolyte minerals calcium, magnesium and sodium, which work together for good nerve and muscle function. A diet high in vegetables and other whole foods should regulate the body's supplies naturally, but a deficiency in potassium is occasionally a problem. Electrolyte minerals, which are also contained in figs, should be kept up in pregnancy to prevent blood pressure from rising and becoming a complication.

- Contain high levels of potassium and other electrolyte minerals that control nerve and muscle function.
- Help prevent common second trimester symptoms such as fatigue, muscle cramps and constipation.
- Help prevent high blood pressure that may result in pre-eclampsia later in pregnancy.

Practical tips:
As snacks, dried figs can help provide a steady source of slow-release sugar, to regulate energy levels and curb sugar cravings. A few figs a day will keep you regular but don't eat in excess, because they are very sweet and may even cause potassium-depleting diarrhoea if you overindulge.

DID YOU KNOW?
Dried figs contain the highest fibre levels of any fruit and a protein-digesting latex called ficin. Snacking on them is a simple way to ward off pregnancy constipation.

MAJOR NUTRIENTS PER 25 G/1 oz DRIED FIGS

Kcalories	75
Total fat	0.28 g
Protein	0.99 g
Carbohydrate	19.16 g
Fibre	2.9 g
Calcium	49 mg
Magnesium	20 mg
Potassium	204 mg
Iron	0.61 mg

Baked stuffed honey figs

SERVES 4 (A) (N) (V)

150 ml/5 fl oz fresh orange juice
6 tsp Greek honey
12 ready-to-eat dried figs
40 g/1½ oz shelled pistachio nuts,
    finely chopped
25 g/1 oz ready-to-eat dried
    apricots, very finely chopped
1 tsp sesame seeds
Greek-style yogurt, to serve

Method

1 Preheat the oven to 180°C/350°F/Gas Mark 4. Put the orange juice and 4 teaspoons of the honey in a saucepan and heat gently until the honey has dissolved. Add the figs and simmer for 10 minutes, or until softened. Remove from the heat and leave the figs to cool in the liquid.

2 Meanwhile, prepare the filling. Put the nuts, apricots, sesame seeds and remaining 2 teaspoons of honey in a bowl and mix well.

3 Using a slotted spoon, remove the figs from the cooking liquid and reserve. Cut a slit at the top of each fig, where the stem joins. Using your fingers, plump up the figs and stuff each fig with about 1 teaspoon of the filling mixture. Close the top of each fig and place in an ovenproof dish. Pour over the reserved cooking liquid.

4 Bake the figs in the preheated oven for 10 minutes, or until hot. Serve warm, or cold, with the sauce and Greek-style yogurt.

44 STRAWBERRIES

Strawberries contain many elements that aid circulation, supporting the needs of a growing baby in the second trimester as it demands an increased supply of blood.

A baby's need for oxygen and nutrients, delivered via the blood, increases during this rapid stage of growth. This process must be supported by iron, necessary to make haemoglobin in blood, but often forgotten is vitamin C, which the body needs in order for iron to be absorbed. The vitamin C in strawberries also supports immunity, meaning a mother can ward off infection and be less likely to need medication and, together with the folate (folic acid) in this fruit, it is needed to make new cells for both mother and baby, and help prevent stretch marks. Along with the protective antioxidant proanthocyanidins in strawberries, vitamin C keeps the circulation flowing and blood vessels intact to help reduce common second trimester symptoms, such as nosebleeds, easy bruising, haemorrhoids and varicose veins, all of which may result from higher blood volume.

- Vitamin C enables absorption of the iron needed to produce new red blood cells to nourish the baby.
- Contain vitamin C and folate to aid new growth for the foetus, and also help prevent or lessen stretch marks.
- Proanthocyanidins work with vitamin C to help prevent symptoms of poor circulation, such as nosebleeds and haemorrhoids.

Practical tips:
To boost antioxidant levels, add strawberries as a sweet treat to porridge, yogurt or cereal. Remove the stem cap just before eating to preserve the high vitamin C content.

DID YOU KNOW?
The old wives' tale that eating strawberries during pregnancy causes strawberry marks has absolutely no basis in truth.

MAJOR NUTRIENTS PER 100 G/3½ OZ STRAWBERRIES

Kcalories	32
Total fat	0.3 g
Protein	0.67 g
Carbohydrate	7.68 g
Fibre	2 g
Vitamin C	58.8 mg
Potassium	153 mg
Folate	24 mcg
Lutein/Zeaxanthin	26 mcg

Breakfast berry smoothie

SERVES 1–2 (G) (A) (V) (Q)

200 g/7 oz strawberries, hulled
100 g/3½ oz raspberries
150 ml/5 fl oz milk
40 g/1½ oz unsweetened muesli

Method

1 Reserve a strawberry for decoration, then place all the ingredients in a food processor or blender and process until almost smooth. Pour into glasses, top each smoothie with half a strawberry and serve.

45

CHEDDAR CHEESE

Cheese can be a healthy addition to the diet during pregnancy when eaten with lots of vegetables, omega-3 fatty acids and very little refined sugar.

MAJOR NUTRIENTS PER 100 G/3½ OZ CHEDDAR CHEESE

Kcalories	403
Total fat	106 g
Saturated fat	21.09 g
Monounsaturated fat	9.39 g
Protein	24.9 g
Carbohydrate	1.28 g
Fibre	0 g
Vitamin B2	0.38 mg
Vitamin B5	0.41 mg
Vitamin B12	0.83 mcg
Vitamin A	1,002 IU
Vitamin D	12 IU
Choline	16.5 mg
Calcium	721 mg
Magnesium	28 mg
Potassium	98 mg
Iron	0.68 mg
Zinc	3.11 mg
Selenium	13.9 mcg

Cheese is high in saturated fat, the hard fat that has been so maligned in recent years. However, some intake of saturated fat is essential in order to enable cells to communicate with one another and to enhance our immunity against disease. Saturated fat is also needed to lend vital energy to the heart – it keeps the mother's pumping that extra blood around, while allowing the baby's to grow strong. Meanwhile, the calcium in cheese helps regulate the heartbeat, and the phosphorus and vitamin A also present allow the calcium to be moved easily into bone. The amino acid tryptophan in cheese enables us to make the 'happy' brain chemical serotonin, and zinc is also crucial for a positive outlook. Quality protein and B vitamins help to prevent the depression and moodiness that can sometimes accompany pregnancy.

- Saturated fat within a healthy diet supports nerve function, immunity and heart health for both mother and baby.
- Phosphorus and vitamin A all help to lock essential calcium into new bone growth.
- Tryptophan, the B vitamins and protein are important mood foods that help prevent pregnancy blues and moodiness.

Practical tips:
For taste and health choose mature Cheddar cheese and eat in small amounts. When aged, the bacterial process cultivates fermenting bacteria and this can help your digestion.

Broccoli and cheese soup

SERVES 6   (G)(A)(V)(Q)

25 g/1 oz butter

1 onion, chopped

2 tsp chopped fresh tarragon,
plus extra to garnish

450 g/1 lb potatoes, peeled and
grated

1.7 litres/3 pints vegetable stock

700 g/1 lb 9 oz broccoli, cut into
small florets

175 g/6 oz Cheddar cheese, grated

1 tbsp chopped fresh parsley

pepper

Method

1 Melt the butter in a large, heavy-based saucepan. Add the onion
and cook, stirring occasionally, for 5 minutes, until softened. Add
the tarragon with the potatoes, season with pepper to taste and mix
well. Pour in just enough of the stock to cover and bring to the boil.
Reduce the heat, cover, and simmer for 10 minutes.

2 Meanwhile, bring the remaining stock to the boil in another
saucepan. Add the broccoli and cook for 6–8 minutes, until
just tender.

3 Remove both pans from the heat, leave to cool slightly, then ladle
the contents of both into a food processor or blender. Process
until smooth, then pour the mixture into a clean saucepan. Stir
the cheese into the pan with the parsley and heat gently to warm
through, but do not allow the soup to boil. Ladle into warmed soup
bowls, garnish with tarragon and serve immediately.

46

SPRING ONIONS

Spring onions are rich sources of cleansing sulphur. Like other alliums, including leeks and garlic, they help to keep toxins away from the baby as it grows.

The mineral sulphur has multiple detoxifying effects. It helps carry waste products out of both the mother's cells and the baby's, enabling nutrients to move in. It also promotes liver detoxification, thereby sweeping out toxic metals from the body. Sulphur, alongside the vitamin C and vitamin A present, is also needed to produce the collagen needed for skin and organs to be able to grow. Spring onions contain much more vitamin K than normal white onions, and this is needed along with the phosphorus content to allow calcium to form new bone. Eating onions may also prevent colds, a particular advantage at this stage, when the mucous membranes may be prone to swelling, causing nasal congestion and hampering the body's attempts to recover from infection.

- Cleansing sulphur removes toxins from cells via the liver, and facilitates an improved uptake of nutrients.
- Sulphur, vitamins C and A help generate collagen for new growth.
- Vitamin K and phosphorus aid mineralization of calcium into bone.
- Onions help prevent coughs and colds, which can be harder to shift during pregnancy.

Practical tips:
All of the spring onion can be eaten. Chopped finely and added to stir-fries, salads or as a garnish for soups and stews, they provide refreshing crunch and bite. Choose bunches with clean white bulbs and leaves that look alive and healthy.

DID YOU KNOW?

Some women crave onions during pregnancy, while others cannot stand the smell or suddenly discover that they cause digestive upsets or indigestion. The milder spring onion may be more tolerated than other varieties.

MAJOR NUTRIENTS PER 1 TBSP CHOPPED SPRING ONIONS

Kcalories	5
Total fat	0.03 g
Protein	0.27 g
Carbohydrate	1.10 g
Fibre	0.4 g
Vitamin C	2.8 mg
Vitamin A	150 IU
Vitamin K	31.1 mcg
Potassium	41 mg
Lutein/Zeaxanthin	171 mcg

Tomato and spring onion twister

SERVES 1–2   (G) (A) (N) (V) (Q)

3 tomatoes

2 spring onions, trimmed

25 g/1 oz fresh basil

1 garlic clove

ice cubes, to serve

shredded spring onions, to garnish

Method

1 Place one tomato in a food processor or blender and firmly pack in the onions, basil and garlic, then top with the remaining tomatoes. Process all the ingredients, then pour into glasses with ice cubes. Top with shredded spring onions and serve.

47

SESAME SEEDS

Sesame seeds are bundles of nutritional goodness. They make it easy to add essential fatty acids, antioxidants and minerals to any meal.

The rich essential fatty acids sesame seeds contain support collagen production, promoting healthy all-round growth, and the fat-soluble nutrients vitamins A and E protect these fatty acids and the baby's eyes, brain, heart and skin from damage. Sesamin and sesamolin, substances only found in sesame seeds, actually revitalize the vitamin E so that it can be used over again, while zinc transports vitamin A around the body and ensures the baby's lungs develop properly. Boasting the highest phytosterol content of any food, sesame seeds help keep the immune system regulated and reduce the risk of allergic reactions and sensitivities.

- Essential fatty acids, vitamin A and E protect and support the growth of fatty areas in the baby's body.
- Sesamin and sesamolin revitalize vitamin E.
- Zinc takes vitamin A to where it is needed and supports lung development.
- Contain phytosterols that help prevent harmful inflammation.

DID YOU KNOW?

Any information you may have heard about sesame seeds leading to miscarriage is erroneous and based on old wives' tales about 'heating the body'.

MAJOR NUTRIENTS PER 15 G/½ oz SESAME SEEDS, UNHULLED

Kcalories	86
Total fat	7.45 g
Monounsaturated fat	2.81 g
Omega-3 fatty acids	56.4 mg
Omega-6 fatty acids	3,205.8 mg
Protein	2.66 g
Carbohydrate	3.52 g
Fibre	1.8 g
Vitamin B3	0.68 mg
Vitamin B6	0.12 mg
Calcium	146 mg
Magnesium	53 mg
Iron	2.18 mg
Zinc	1.16 mg
Selenium	5.2 mcg

Practical tips:

Choose the unhulled seeds if possible, in order to benefit from the fibre, oils, fat-soluble vitamins and minerals in the hull. Never cook with sesame seeds because the delicate essential fatty acids are easily damaged by heat. Sprinkle over stir-fries just before serving, and over salads and steamed vegetables. Tahini (sesame paste) has the added benefits of garlic and olive oil.

Golden tofu noodles with sesame seeds

SERVES 2　(G) (A) (V)

2 tsp virgin coconut oil

5 tbsp tamari

1 tbsp honey

5-cm/2-inch piece fresh ginger,
peeled and finely chopped

300 g/10½ oz firm tofu, drained,
patted dry and cut into slices
1 cm/½ inch thick

175 g/6 oz soba noodles

1 tsp sesame oil

1 carrot, diced

3 radishes, sliced into rounds

2 spring onions, diagonally sliced

25 g/1 oz mangetout, diagonally
sliced

small handful fresh coriander
leaves, chopped

1 tsp sesame seeds

pepper

Method

1 Preheat the oven to 190°C/375°C/Gas Mark 5. Heat the coconut oil, 3 tablespoons of the tamari, the honey and half of the ginger in a wide saucepan, stirring until combined. Remove from the heat and add the tofu, spoon the tamari mixture over until coated, then set aside for 10 minutes.

2 Arrange the tofu on a non-stick baking tray and roast for 20–25 minutes, turning once, until golden.

3 Meanwhile, cook the noodles in gently boiling water for 5 minutes, or according to packet instructions, until tender. Drain then refresh under cold running water until cool, then transfer to a bowl. Mix together the remaining tamari, ginger and sesame oil. Season with pepper and pour over the noodles.

4 Add the carrot, radishes, spring onions, mangetout and coriander to the noodles. Turn the noodles gently until everything is combined.

5 To serve, divide the noodles between two plates then scatter over the sesame seeds and top with the tofu.

48 BEETROOT

Beetroot works hard to support growth during pregnancy, while helping reduce the risk of damage to the foetus by protecting DNA and removing toxins.

As one of the richest food sources of folate (folic acid), beetroot encourages the all-round growth of the baby, while betacyanin, the antioxidant pigment that provides the rich colour, helps protect DNA to minimize the risk of defects. Betaine, also present in beetroot, stimulates the liver cells to remove toxins that can interfere with development, and which may cause nausea, fatigue and headaches. Beetroot contains a healthy dose of the mineral potassium which helps keep blood pressure and fluid balance regulated. The trace mineral silica allows calcium to be effectively incorporated into new bone growth.

- One of the best folate food sources to promote all growth.
- Betacyanin and betaine help protect DNA from damage to minimize the risk of growth defects.
- Betaine supports detoxification to help prevent headaches, tiredness and nausea.
- Potassium helps regulate blood pressure and may help prevent water retention.
- Silica works with other bone nutrients to promote skeletal health in mother and baby.

Practical tips:
Look for products without added vinegar if you tend to suffer from yeast infections. The fresh root can be steamed or boiled, or roasted in a little olive oil, and is delicious eaten hot or cold.

DID YOU KNOW?

In the 16th century, beetroot was given as a 'blood builder' to people who looked pale. Today we would say its high iron content was being used to treat anaemia. It can be eaten during pregnancy to keep iron stores up.

MAJOR NUTRIENTS PER 100 G/3½ OZ BEETROOT

Kcalories	43
Total fat	0.17 g
Protein	1.61 g
Carbohydrate	9.56 g
Fibre	2.8 g
Vitamin B3	0.33 mg
Vitamin B5	0.16 mg
Folate	109 mcg
Calcium	16 mg
Magnesium	23 mg
Potassium	325 mg
Iron	0.8 mg
Selenium	0.7 mcg
Betaine	128.7 mg

Red cabbage and beetroot slaw

SERVES 4   (G) (A) (V) (Q)

350 g/12 oz red cabbage, finely
    shredded
175 g/6 oz cooked beetroot, sliced
    into thin matchsticks
1 apple, cored and thinly sliced
1 tbsp lemon juice
1 tbsp sunflower seeds
1 tbsp pumpkin seeds
salt and pepper

Dressing

5 tbsp Greek-style yogurt
1 tbsp red wine vinegar
pepper

Method

1 Place the cabbage, beetroot and apple slices in a large bowl. Add the lemon juice and mix well.

2 To make the dressing, place the yogurt and red wine vinegar in a bowl and mix together until smooth. Pour over the salad and stir well. Season with pepper, cover, and chill in the refrigerator for at least 1 hour.

3 Stir the salad thoroughly and adjust the seasoning to taste. Sprinkle with the sunflower and pumpkin seeds just before serving.

49 CHICKPEAS

Chickpeas contain protein, complex carbohydrates, fibre, B vitamins and minerals to support aspects of growth, energy, immunity and detoxification.

DID YOU KNOW?

Chickpeas are consistently associated with lowered rates of heart disease across all cultures that eat them regularly. This may be useful in pregnancy when blood pressure tends to rise and increased circulation creates more work for your heart.

MAJOR NUTRIENTS PER 100 G/3½ OZ CHICKPEAS, UNCOOKED

Kcalories	364
Total fat	6.04 g
Protein	19.3 g
Carbohydrate	60.65 g
Vitamin B3	1.54 mg
Vitamin B5	1.59 mg
Folate	557 mcg
Choline	95.2 mg
Calcium	105 mg
Magnesium	115 mg
Potassium	875 mg
Iron	6.24 mg
Selenium	13.9 mcg
Zinc	0.49 mg
Manganese	2.2 mg

Chickpeas and other legumes and beans are an important way to boost increased pregnancy protein needs for your baby's growth. Achieving these through plant as well as animal sources, like meat, fish and eggs, helps to maintain the correct, slightly alkaline balance in your body. This can ensure your body keeps good fluid balance and detoxification processes at a time of increased need. The slow-release complex carbohydrates and B vitamins in chickpeas help to regulate energy and appetite to reduce the urge for quick-fix sugary foods that may exacerbate the energy dips and mood swings common in pregnancy. A good spread of minerals offers iron for red blood cell production, calcium, magnesium and manganese for your baby's skeletal development, and selenium and zinc for antioxidant protection for you and your baby.

- Protein for optimal growth of your baby and in an alkaline form to help maintain fluid balance and detoxification.
- Carbohydrates, fibre and B vitamins ensure sustained energy levels to help reduce sugar cravings and energy and mood lows.
- Good mineral levels support growth and immune protection.

Practical tips:
Dried chickpeas can take a lot of soaking (between 12 and 24 hours) to prepare them for cooking, so are easiest used from cans or jars. They are the main ingredient in hummus, easily prepared by blending with garlic, tahini, olive oil and lemon juice.

Chickpea and potato soup

SERVES 4   (G) (B) (A) (V)

1 tbsp olive oil

1 large onion, finely chopped

2–3 garlic cloves, finely chopped
or crushed

1 carrot, quartered and thinly sliced

350 g/12 oz potatoes, diced

¼ tsp garam masala

¼ tsp mild curry powder

400 g/14 oz canned chopped
tomatoes

850 ml/1½ pints water

¼ tsp chilli powder, or to taste
(optional)

pinch of salt

400 g/14 oz canned chickpeas,
drained and rinsed

85 g/3 oz fresh or frozen peas

pepper

chopped fresh coriander, to garnish

Method

1 Heat the olive oil in a large saucepan over a medium heat. Add the onion and garlic and cook, stirring occasionally, for 3–4 minutes, until the onion is beginning to soften. Add the carrot, potatoes, garam masala and curry powder and continue cooking for 1–2 minutes.

2 Add the tomatoes, water and chilli powder, if using, with the salt. Reduce the heat, cover and simmer for 30 minutes, stirring occasionally.

3 Add the chickpeas and peas to the pan, then continue cooking for about 15 minutes, or until all the vegetables are tender. Taste the soup and adjust the seasoning, if necessary, adding a little more chilli powder if you like. Ladle into warmed soup bowls, sprinkle with chopped coriander and serve immediately.

50 TROUT

Trout supplies the healthy levels of fat needed to support a growing bump and also contribute to the fat developing under the baby's skin.

As an oily fish, the fats in trout are healthy omega-3 fatty acids. There are two kinds of omega-3 fatty acids: EPA, which supports heart and circulatory functions, and DHA, which is needed in high levels in the brain, central nervous system and eyes. Some studies suggest that mothers with the highest levels of omega-3 fatty acids in their bodies have children who show better brain development up until the age of two, and even beyond, though the evidence is not conclusive. Our main source of vitamin D is sunlight but food sources, such as trout, help keep up levels when light exposure is low, so that we receive vitamin D's positive effects on mood, bone health and hormone levels. The B vitamins and omega-3 fatty acids also play vital roles in mood and energy regulation, helping to limit pregnancy blues and fatigue.

- Contains healthy oils that build up protective fat layers.
- Omega-3 fatty acids support heart, circulation, brain, eye and motor functions in the developing baby.
- High levels of DHA in the diet may result in children with more advanced cognitive skills.
- Vitamin D, the B vitamins and omega-3 fatty acids maintain mood and energy during pregnancy.

Practical tips:
Trout contains only very low levels of mercury so is an oily fish that is safe to eat during pregnancy, if limited to two portions a week.

DID YOU KNOW?

The pink colour of trout flesh comes from a fatty antioxidant, astaxanthin, that is particularly neuroprotective. Eating trout will therefore help ensure the safety of the baby's brain and nervous system.

MAJOR NUTRIENTS PER 100 G/3½ OZ FRESH TROUT

Kcalories	148
Total fat	6.61 g
Omega-3 fatty acids – EPA	0.2 g
Omega-3 fatty acids – DHA	0.53 g
Protein	20.77 g
Carbohydrate	0 g
Fibre	0 g
Vitamin B1	0.35 mg
Vitamin B3	4.5 mg
Vitamin B5	1.94 mg
Vitamin B12	7.79 mcg
Vitamin D	155 IU

Marinated trout fillets

SERVES 4   (G) (B)

4 trout, cleaned and filleted
lemon wedges, to garnish
green beans and sautéed potatoes,
    to serve

Marinade

4 tsp vegetable oil
juice of ½ lemon
4 fresh fennel sprigs, finely
    chopped, plus extra, to garnish
pepper

Method

1 To make the marinade,
   combine the oil and lemon
   juice in a small bowl and whisk
   together. Stir in the chopped
   fennel and a little pepper,
   to taste.

2 Put the trout fillets in a
   shallow, non-metallic dish.
   Pour over the fennel mixture,
   cover the dish with clingfilm
   and leave to marinate in the
   refrigerator for 30 minutes.

3 Remove the trout from the
   refrigerator and return to
   room temperature. Preheat
   the griddle over a medium
   heat. Transfer the trout to
   the griddle and brush the
   marinade over the fish. Cook
   the fillets for 5 minutes on
   each side, turning once and
   brushing with the remaining
   marinade.

4 Remove the trout from
   the griddle and arrange
   on a serving dish. Garnish
   with fennel sprigs and
   lemon wedges, then serve
   immediately with green beans
   and sautéed potatoes.

51

PINTO BEANS

Pinto beans contain both protein and complex carbohydrates, regulating blood sugar levels, energy and mood, and helping to prevent overeating during this trimester.

MAJOR NUTRIENTS PER 100 G/3½ oz DRIED PINTO BEANS

Kcalories	347
Total fat	1.23 g
Protein	21.42 g
Carbohydrate	62.55 g
Fibre	15.5 g
Vitamin B1	0.72 mg
Vitamin B2	0.21 mg
Vitamin B3	1.17 mg
Vitamin B5	0.79 mg
Vitamin B6	0.47 mg
Folate	525 mcg
Choline	66.2 mg
Calcium	113 mg
Magnesium	176 mg
Potassium	1,393 mg
Zinc	2.28 mg
Selenium	27.9 mcg

Pinto beans have a healthy all-round B-vitamin profile, enabling them to unlock their energy potential, and good levels of the lesser-known B-vitamin choline in particular, which helps move fats through the liver and prevent nausea and bloating. Also included in the B vitamins is folate (folic acid), necessary for growth and red blood cell production throughout pregnancy. Lower levels of folate in the second trimester have been shown to increase the risk of pre-eclampsia in the third, and are generally associated with lower birth weights. The calcium, magnesium and potassium in pinto beans are electrolyte minerals that support heart, brain and muscle function in both mother and baby.

- Protein, slow-release carbohydrates and the B vitamins regulate pregnancy energy and mood fluctuations.
- Choline helps reduce sickness and fluid retention.
- Folate supports foetal growth and lowers the risk of pre-eclampsia and low birth weight.
- Calcium, magnesium and potassium regulate heart, muscle and brain function.

Practical tips:

As with any bean, they can be used to make soups, stews and to add to salads. They also make great dips. Blend with olive oil, garlic and lemon, or even grapefruit juice. Serve with vegetable sticks or crackers as a convenient snack.

Vegetarian paella

SERVES 4–6 (G) (B) (A) (V)

½ tsp saffron strands

2 tbsp hot water

6 tbsp olive oil

1 onion, sliced

3 garlic cloves, crushed

1 red pepper, deseeded and sliced

1 orange pepper, deseeded and sliced

1 large aubergine, cubed

200 g/7 oz medium-grain paella rice

600 ml/1 pint vegetable stock

450 g/1 lb tomatoes, peeled and chopped

115 g/4 oz button mushrooms, sliced

115 g/4 oz green beans, halved

400 g/14 oz canned pinto beans

pepper

Method

1 Put the saffron strands and water in a small bowl and let them infuse for a few minutes.

2 Meanwhile, heat the oil in a paella pan or wide, shallow frying pan and cook the onion over a medium heat, stirring, for 2–3 minutes, or until softened. Add the garlic, peppers and aubergine and cook, stirring frequently, for 5 minutes.

3 Add the rice and cook, stirring constantly, for 1 minute, or until glossy and coated. Pour in the stock and add the tomatoes, saffron and its soaking water, and pepper to taste. Bring to a boil, then reduce the heat and let simmer, shaking the pan frequently and stirring occasionally, for 15 minutes.

4 Stir in the mushrooms, green beans and the pinto beans with their can juices. Cook for a further 10 minutes, then serve immediately.

52 PECANS

Nuts provide the best fat, fibre and carbohydrate package of any food. Pecans are also high in antioxidants and B vitamins to ensure the health of the baby.

At this stage, the baby is developing insulating fat under the skin and fats are needed to supply this, as well as to help develop the foetal organs. The omega-9 fatty acids (monounsaturated fat) in pecans protect the baby's heart, while the magnesium and potassium help it beat regularly. The trace mineral manganese and the omega-3 fatty acids in these nuts are involved in developing the baby's brain structure. Meanwhile the protein provided, together with manganese, folate (folic acid) and zinc allow the baby's body, from its tendons and ligaments to fingers and toes, to develop and grow.

- Provides energy and antioxidant protection against cell damage.
- Quality fats create a healthy fatty layer beneath the baby's skin.
- Monounsaturated fats, magnesium and potassium ensure heart health.
- Manganese and omega-3 fatty acids support the baby's brain chemistry and development.
- Protein, manganese, folate and zinc allow the baby's body structures to mature correctly.

Practical tips:
Snack on a handful of pecans to help prevent blood sugar lows that can lead to dizziness or fainting. Whizz in the blender to make an alternative to peanut butter. Avoid roasted nuts or cooking with pecans, because the essential fatty acids can be damaged.

DID YOU KNOW?

Pecans not only regulate blood sugar but also provide magnesium, low levels of which can lead to unstoppable cravings for chocolate.

MAJOR NUTRIENTS PER 25 G/1 oz PECANS

Kcalories	207
Total fat	21.6 g
Monounsaturated fat	12.2 g
Omega-3 fatty acids	295 mg
Omega-6 fatty acids	6,189 mg
Protein	2.7 g
Carbohydrate	4.15 g
Fibre	2.8 g
Vitamin B1	0.19 mg
Vitamin B3	0.35 mg
Vitamin B5	0.25 mg
Folate	55 mcg
Magnesium	36 mg
Potassium	123 mg
Iron	1.4 mg
Manganese	1.25 mg
Zinc	1.25 mg
Phytosterols	32 mg

Pear, pecan and watercress salad

SERVES 2   Ⓖ Ⓑ Ⓐ Ⓥ Ⓠ

*1 pear, halved, cored and thinly
  sliced*

1 tsp lemon juice

50 g/1¾ oz watercress

25 g/1 oz pecan halves

Dressing

2 tbsp extra virgin olive oil

½ tsp clear honey

½ tsp wholegrain mustard

2 tsp lemon juice

salt and pepper

Method

1 Toss the pear slices in the lemon juice to prevent them browning.
2 Place the watercress in a large, shallow serving bowl and top with the pear. Scatter over the pecans.
3 To make the dressing, mix together the oil, honey, mustard and lemon juice. Season with salt and pepper, then drizzle the dressing over the salad before serving.

53 CUCUMBER

Cucumber makes a refreshing, cooling and soothing food at a time when dehydration can quickly lead to tiredness, headaches and fluid retention.

One of cucumber's main benefits is its high water content, which together with the potassium and magnesium make it instantly hydrating and an effective tool in the prevention of high blood pressure. The trace mineral silica in cucumber provides support to the body's skin structures and will ease the expansion of skin around the bump as it grows. The potassium, vitamin C and caffeic acid in cucumber help prevent any excess fluid around the ankles, wrists, fingers and eyes. Caffeic acid, which has no relation to caffeine, is an antioxidant that displays anti-inflammatory and immune-regulating properties. It is particularly useful as an anti-fungal, helping prevent yeast infections in pregnancy that can be passed later to the child via the birth canal or if breastfeeding.

- Contains water, potassium and magnesium, all of which are hydrating and help regulate blood pressure.
- Silica supports the structure of skin as it grows and expands.
- Potassium, vitamin C and caffeic acid may have a positive effect on pregnancy puffiness.
- Caffeic acid supports immunity, reduces inflammation and helps prevent fungal infection.

Practical tips:
Use cucumber slices as an effective remedy for tired and puffy eyes. To alleviate fluid retention, make an easy drink by blending cucumber with water and mint.

DID YOU KNOW?

Cucumber, and other foods with anti-inflammatory properties, can help ease aches and pains in pregnancy, such as the twinges felt in the second trimester as the ribcage expands to accommodate the baby.

MAJOR NUTRIENTS PER 100 G/3½ OZ CUCUMBER, WITH PEEL

Kcalories	16
Total fat	0.11 g
Protein	0.65 g
Carbohydrate	3.63 g
Fibre	0.5 g
Vitamin C	2.8 mg
Vitamin B5	0.26 mg
Magnesium	13 mg
Potassium	147 mg

Cucumber and tomato soup

SERVES 6   (G) (A) (N) (V)

4 tomatoes, peeled and deseeded

10-cm/4-inch piece of cucumber, peeled and deseeded

2 spring onions, green part only, chopped

1.5 kg/3 lb 5 oz watermelon, rind removed and deseeded

1 tbsp chopped fresh mint

salt and pepper

fresh mint sprigs, to garnish

Method

1 Put the tomatoes into a blender or food processor and, with the motor running, add the cucumber, spring onions, watermelon and mint. Season to taste with salt and pepper and blend until smooth.

2 If you are not using a blender or food processor, push the watermelon through a sieve. Dice the tomatoes and add them to the melon mixture with the mint. Finely chop the cucumber and spring onions and add to the mixture.

3 Chill the soup overnight in the refrigerator. Check the seasoning and transfer to a serving dish. Garnish with the mint sprigs and serve.

54 GRAPEFRUIT

Although grapefruit tastes very acidic, once processed in the body it has a potent alkalizing effect that helps maintain the best possible environment for the baby.

Grapefruit helps our natural pH levels stay on track so that all processes can work efficiently. For the baby, this means a healthy exchange of nutrients and oxygen via the placenta. Vitamin C and bioflavonoids, including limonene, are antioxidants found in the white pith of grapefruit that help regulate the immune system and prevent sensitivities or intolerances being passed on to the baby. Along with selenium and the B vitamins in the fruit, these antioxidants help the liver process and expel toxins that may be harmful to a foetus. If you are on any medications, however, you should discuss grapefruit consumption with your doctor before including it in your diet because the substance naringin, found in the fruit, can affect the way drugs are metabolized.

- Alkalizing action counters the stressful effects of life's demands, pollution and the occasional less-than-healthy foodstuff.
- Vitamin C and bioflavonoids regulate immunity, enabling the mother to pass on the benefits to her child.
- Vitamin C, limonene, selenium and the B vitamins help liver detoxification to keep harmful substances away from the baby.

Practical tips:
Grapefruit is a natural and refreshing convenience food. Halve, or peel and eat like an orange. If you don't like too sour a taste, try the pink variety because it is sweeter.

DID YOU KNOW?

Sour foods such as grapefruit can stimulate the digestive processes to help break down and absorb any food eaten afterwards. They are a helpful starter when an expanding belly makes digestion harder.

MAJOR NUTRIENTS PER MEDIUM-SIZED HALF GRAPEFRUIT

Kcalories	39
Total fat	0.12 g
Protein	0.81 g
Carbohydrate	9.92 g
Fibre	1.3 g
Vitamin C	39.3 mg
Vitamin B3	0.32 mg
Vitamin B5	0.33 mg
Vitamin A	39 IU mcg
Potassium	175 mg
Selenium	1.7 mcg

Chicken and grapefruit salad

SERVES 4   (G) (A)

2 skinless, boneless chicken
    breasts, about 175 g/6 oz each

1 bouquet garni

few black peppercorns

2 pink grapefruit

3 Little Gem lettuces, separated
    into leaves

1 head chicory, separated into
    leaves

fresh chervil sprigs, to garnish

Dressing

1 tbsp light olive oil

3 tbsp Greek-style yogurt

1 tsp wholegrain mustard

1 tbsp chopped fresh chervil

pepper

Method

1 Place the chicken in a large saucepan and pour over enough water
   to cover. Add the bouquet garni and peppercorns and bring to
   a gentle simmer. Cover and simmer for 25–30 minutes, until just
   cooked through. Leave the chicken to cool in the liquid.

2 Using a serrated knife, cut away the peel and pith from the
   grapefruit. Holding the fruit over a bowl to catch any juice, segment
   the flesh. Reserve 2 tablespoons of the juice.

3 Toss the salad leaves in a bowl with the grapefruit segments.

4 To make the dressing, place all the ingredients in a small bowl with
   the reserved grapefruit juice. Whisk together until the dressing is
   thoroughly blended.

5 Drain the poached chicken and pat dry with kitchen paper. Tear into
   bite-sized strips or thinly slice. Arrange on top of the salad. Drizzle
   over the dressing and garnish with chervil sprigs.

55 PARSLEY

Parsley contains a potent cocktail of antioxidants that provide protection from free radical damage to every cell of both mother and baby's growing body.

Parsley contains a mixture of the powerful antioxidants vitamin C, quercetin, luteolin and rutin. They prevent damage from the continual onslaught of free radical damage from pollution and chemicals. They are also antihistamines, naturally bringing down inflammation and helping to prevent associated effects in pregnancy, including pre-eclampsia, bloating and acne. These antioxidants strengthen and tone blood vessels to support blood flow to the baby and help prevent the bruising, varicose veins and haemorrhoids that can become a problem as your pregnancy goes on. Extra antioxidant protection of the baby's nervous system, heart, eyes and skin comes in the form of the carotenoids beta carotene, lutein and zeaxanthin.

- Antioxidants vitamin C, quercetin, luteolin and rutin prevent damage to all body tissues.
- These also bring down inflammation and support circulation to help prevent common pregnancy symptoms, such as acne and haemorrhoids.
- Beta carotene, lutein and zeaxanthin support the health of the baby's eyes, skin, heart and brain.

Practical tips:
The fresh, chopped herb can be added to the end of most dishes for extra greenery and nutrients. It also freezes well. Try adding to smoothies and juices and substitute for basil in pesto.

DID YOU KNOW?

Supplements of parsley oil should be avoided in pregnancy as they can cause early contractions, but the culinary use of all commonly-used fresh or dried herbs is highly beneficial.

MAJOR NUTRIENTS PER 15 G/½ OZ PARSLEY

Kcalories	3
Total fat	0.01 g
Protein	0.5 g
Carbohydrate	1 g
Fibre	0.5 g
Vitamin C	20 mg
Folate	23 mcg
Calcium	21 mg
Magnesium	8 mg
Potassium	83 mg
Iron	0.9 mg
Beta carotene	758 mcg
Lutein/Zeaxanthin	834 mcg

Baked fish with chimichurro sauce

SERVES 2   (G) (B) (A) (Q)

extra virgin olive oil, for oiling

2 x 175 g/6 oz thick white fish
   fillets, such as line-caught cod,
   haddock or pollack

4 slices lemon

salad leaves

pepper

Chimichurro sauce

large handful fresh flat-leaf parsley,
   leaves removed

1 large garlic clove

4 tbsp extra virgin olive oil

1 tsp dried oregano

½ tsp ground cumin

large pinch of dried chilli flakes

Method

1 Preheat the oven to 200°C/400°F/Gas Mark 6. Lightly oil 2 pieces of foil with olive oil. Place a fish fillet in the centre of each piece of foil, season with pepper and top with the lemon slices. Fold up the edges of the foil to seal, then place the parcels on a baking sheet. Bake for 15–20 minutes, depending on the thickness of the fillets, until cooked.

2 Meanwhile, to make the chimichurro sauce, put the parsley, garlic, oil, oregano, cumin and chilli in a beaker and mix with a food processor or blender until combined.

3 Remove the fish parcels from the oven, open and discard the lemon slices. Top the fish with the chimichurro sauce and serve with salad leaves.

56

GLOBE ARTICHOKES

Globe artichokes provide an excellent boost of the essential minerals necessary to keep circulation, fluid levels and bone development on track.

The minerals needed for the baby's growth and the mother's continuing health are called essential because they have to be obtained through the diet. If the diet doesn't provide enough, the body will make the baby its priority and the mother will suffer deficiency symptoms. Artichokes provide a good balance of calcium and magnesium, a lack of which can affect a mother's bone and tooth health and show up in symptoms such as muscle cramps, headaches and insomnia. An inadequate intake of potassium, also present in artichoke, will similarly lead to fatigue and muscle weakness. Artichokes also contain a substance called cynarin, which acts both as a mild laxative and increases bile flow from the liver to aid digestion and detoxification. The bioflavonoid apigenin in artichoke helps relax blood vessels and keep blood pressure within safe levels.

- Calcium and magnesium protect mother and baby's bone health, while relieving muscle aches and anxiety symptoms.
- Potassium wards off pregnancy fatigue and weakened muscles.
- Cynarin is a natural digestive aid and detoxification agent.
- Apigenin is a natural relaxant that eases blood vessels, preventing blood pressure from rising.

Practical tips:

Cook the fresh globes or, for convenience, add roasted artichoke hearts from deli counters to salads. Rub fresh artichoke with lemon juice as soon as it is prepared to avoid discoloration.

DID YOU KNOW?

Artichoke supplements are not advised during pregnancy because the concentrated extract detoxifies the body too intensely. However it is perfectly safe to include artichokes naturally in the diet at this time.

MAJOR NUTRIENTS PER MEDIUM-SIZED GLOBE ARTICHOKE

Kcalories	60
Total fat	0 g
Protein	4.2 g
Carbohydrate	13.4 g
Fibre	6.5 g
Vitamin C	12 mg
Folate	65 mcg
Calcium	54 mg
Magnesium	72 mg
Potassium	425 mg
Iron	1.5 mg
Lutein/Zeaxanthin	557 mcg

Artichoke and rocket salad

SERVES 4   (G) (A) (V) (Q)

8 baby globe artichokes
juice of 2 lemons
bunch of rocket
3–4 tbsp extra virgin olive oil
115 g/4 oz pecorino cheese
pepper

Method

1 Break off the stem of each artichoke and trim about 2.5 cm/1 inch off the top, depending on how young and small they are. Remove and discard any coarse outer leaves, leaving only the pale, tender inner leaves. Using a teaspoon, scoop out the chokes. Rub each artichoke with lemon juice as soon as it is prepared, to prevent discoloration.

2 Thinly slice the artichokes and place in a salad bowl. Add the rocket, remaining lemon juice and olive oil, season to taste with a little pepper, and toss well.

3 Using a swivel-bladed vegetable peeler, thinly shave the pecorino over the salad then serve immediately.

57 CARROT

The carotenoids that give carrots their vibrant colour give protection to the baby's fatty areas, including the brain, liver, skin and eyes.

Although beta carotene is the best known of the carotenoids, the alpha carotene in carrots also stimulates protective antioxidant action within all fatty areas of the body. All cell walls, organs and tissues incorporate fats and these are continually open to damage. These carotenoids can also be stored in the liver and converted into vitamin A as we need it. Obtaining vitamin A from carrots during pregnancy is risk-free, because carotenes are not toxic if taken in excess, whereas high levels of preformed vitamin A are known to cause genetic mutations. Vitamin A is necessary in the right amount for cellular development, fighting infection and to keep the placenta attached. Vitamin A deficiency in underdeveloped countries has been shown to result in maternal eye problems, lowered immune response and anaemia.

- Beta and alpha carotene prevent damage to the fats incorporated in all mother and baby's cells.
- Carotenes can be converted to vitamin A, vital for cell growth, placenta health and immunity.
- A safe way of ingesting and storing vitamin A.

Practical tips:
Carrots are delicious raw, especially grated in salads, and will then release their starchy sugars more slowly. The fat-soluble carotenoids in carrots need oil present at the time of eating to carry the carotenoids from the digestive tract into the bloodstream.

DID YOU KNOW?

The carotenoids in carrots are particularly renowned for their heart protective effects – a bonus in pregnancy when your heart has to work much harder to pump blood to your baby and its volume increases.

MAJOR NUTRIENTS PER 100 G/3½ OZ CARROTS

Kcalories	41
Total fat	0.24 g
Protein	0.93 g
Carbohydrate	9.58 g
Fibre	2.8 g
Vitamin C	5.9 mg
Vitamin A	16,706 IU
Potassium	320 mg
Beta carotene	8,285 mcg
Alpha carotene	3,477 mcg

Creamy carrot and parsnip soup

SERVES 4 (B) (A) (V)

4 tbsp butter

1 large onion, chopped

450 g/1 lb carrots, chopped

2 large parsnips, chopped

1 tbsp peeled and grated fresh
    ginger

1 tsp grated orange rind

600 ml/1 pint vegetable stock

125 ml/4 fl oz Greek-style yogurt

pepper

sprigs of fresh coriander, to garnish

Method

1 Melt the butter in a large saucepan over a low heat. Add the onion
   and cook, stirring, for 3 minutes, until slightly softened. Add the
   carrots and parsnips, cover, and cook, stirring occasionally, for
   about 15 minutes, until the vegetables have softened a little.

2 Stir in the ginger, orange rind and stock. Bring to the boil, then
   reduce the heat, cover, and simmer for 30–35 minutes, until the
   vegetables are tender. Remove from the heat and leave to cool for
   10 minutes.

3 Transfer the soup to a food processor or blender and process until
   smooth. Return the soup to a clean pan, stir in the yogurt and
   season well with pepper. Warm through gently over a low heat.

4 Remove from the heat and ladle into warmed soup bowls. Garnish
   each bowl with pepper and a sprig of coriander, then serve.

58 BROWN RICE

Choosing to eat rice with its brown outer hull intact makes a fundamental difference to the health benefits that this food provides to both mother and baby.

MAJOR NUTRIENTS PER 100 G/3½ OZ BROWN RICE

Kcalories	370
Total fat	2.92 g
Omega-6 fatty acids	1,000 mg
Protein	7.94 g
Carbohydrate	77.24 g
Fibre	3.5 g
Vitamin B1	0.4 mg
Vitamin B3	5.09 mg
Vitamin B5	1.49 mg
Vitamin B6	0.51 mg
Choline	30.7 mg
Vitamin E	1.2 mg
Magnesium	143 mg
Iron	1.47 mg
Manganese	3.74 mg
Selenium	23.4 mcg
Zinc	2.02 mg

The husk of brown rice is the part that contains the fibre, fats, minerals and vitamins. The fibre is prebiotic, which means that it feeds your beneficial, probiotic digestive bacteria. This is a crucial consideration in pregnancy because it ensures that the mother is producing anti-inflammatory antibodies on the walls of her intestines to prevent infection. The selenium and manganese in brown rice help to make antioxidant enzymes in the liver that both eliminate harmful elements in the body and also increase the action of antioxidants eaten in other food. Selenium can be converted into the coenzyme Q-10, needed alongside the B vitamins to create energy in all cells, especially in the hardworking hearts of mother and baby. The B vitamin choline is needed to make new cell walls, while the vitamin E in brown rice protects these from damage.

- Prebiotic fibre lowers a mother's risk of infection.
- Selenium and manganese make antioxidant enzymes that aid detoxification.
- Selenium makes coenzyme Q-10 to create energy in all cells, including both mother's and baby's hearts.
- Choline and vitamin E enable the creation of new cells.

Practical tips:

Choose long-grain rather than short-grain because it releases its sugars into the body more slowly. Brown basmati rice contains 20 per cent more fibre than other varieties of brown rice.

Vegetarian kedgeree

SERVES 2 (G)(A)(V)

115 g/4 oz brown basmati rice,
   rinsed
1 tsp vegetable bouillon powder
3 cardamom pods, split
85 g/3 oz red split lentils
2 tbsp groundnut oil
25 g/1 oz unsalted butter
1 onion, chopped
3 garlic cloves, chopped
2.5-cm/1-inch piece fresh ginger,
   peeled and grated
1 tsp ground cumin
1 tsp ground coriander
1 tsp turmeric
½ tsp dried chilli flakes (optional)
2 hard-boiled eggs, halved
2 tbsp chopped fresh coriander,
   to garnish
pepper (optional)

Method

1 Put the rice in a saucepan and pour in sufficient water to cover by
   1 cm/½ inch. Bring to the boil, stir in the vegetable bouillon and
   cardamom, then reduce the heat to its lowest setting and cover with
   a tight-fitting lid. Simmer the rice for 25 minutes, or until the water
   is absorbed and the grains are tender. Remove from the heat and
   leave to stand.

2 Meanwhile, put the lentils in a second pan, cover with water and
   bring to the boil. Reduce the heat, part-cover, and simmer for
   12–15 minutes, until tender. Drain well.

3 Heat the oil and butter in a large sauté pan and fry the onion for
   6 minutes, until softened. Add the garlic, ginger and spices and
   cook for another minute. Add the rice and lentils to the pan and stir
   until combined. Season with pepper, if not using the chilli flakes.

4 Divide the rice mixture between two bowls and top each serving
   with a hard-boiled egg and fresh coriander, to garnish.

59

KALE

When we chew kale, or other brassicas such as broccoli and cabbage, they release sulphoraphanes, potent chemicals that boost the body's ability to remove toxins.

Vitamin E can help preserve the elasticity of a woman's skin as her belly and breasts expand. It is also known to support pregnancy generally; premature babies often show low vitamin E levels. Kale is an excellent source of vitamin K, which is involved in bone growth and needed to make thrombin, the substance that allows blood to clot. Kale supplies vitamin C, too, which is an important co-factor in the production of the oestrogen and progesterone that maintain pregnancy. Very high levels of the carotenoids beta carotene, lutein and zeaxanthin in kale promote the optimal health of the baby's internal organs and eyes. They also protect the placenta from the toxins it holds back from the baby.

- Vitamin E helps prevent stretch marks and promotes a healthy full-term pregnancy.
- Vitamin K helps the baby's bones grow and reduces future risk of internal bleeding.
- Vitamin C is needed to produce the pregnancy hormones that sustain pregnancy.
- Contains sulphoraphanes and carotenoids that protect the placenta and the baby from toxic damage.

Practical tips:
To retain the most goodness, steam or stir-fry rather than boil, and chop the leaves at the very last moment. Kale can also be made into crisps by baking in pieces for 5–7 minutes.

DID YOU KNOW?
The indole-3-carbinole in brassicas promotes DNA repair and may stop cancer-cell growth. This action can be transmitted from mother to baby and may help prevent cancers in children later on.

MAJOR NUTRIENTS PER 100 G/3½ OZ KALE

Kcalories	50
Total fat	0.7 g
Protein	3.3 g
Carbohydrate	10 g
Fibre	2 g
Vitamin C	120 mg
Vitamin E	1.7 mg
Vitamin K	817 mcg
Folate	29 mcg
Calcium	135 mg
Magnesium	34 mg
Potassium	447 mg
Iron	1.7 mg
Beta carotene	9,226 mcg
Lutein/Zeaxanthin	39,550 mcg

Beans and greens stew

SERVES 4   (G) (A) (V)

250 g/9 oz dried haricot or
   cannellini beans, soaked
   overnight
1 tbsp olive oil
2 onions, finely chopped
4 garlic cloves, finely chopped
1 celery stick, thinly sliced
2 carrots, halved and thinly sliced
1.2 litres/2 pints water
¼ tsp dried thyme
¼ tsp dried marjoram
1 bay leaf
125 g/4½ oz kale
pepper

Method

1 Drain the beans, put them in a saucepan and add enough cold water to cover by 5 cm/ 2 inches. Bring to the boil and boil for 10 minutes. Drain and rinse well.

2 Heat the oil in a large saucepan over a medium heat. Add the onions and cook, covered, for 3–4 minutes, stirring occasionally, until the onions are just softened. Add the garlic, celery and carrots, and continue cooking for 2 minutes.

3 Add the water, drained beans, thyme, marjoram and bay leaf and bring to the boil. When the mixture begins to bubble, reduce the heat to low. Cover and simmer gently, stirring occasionally, for about 1¼ hours, until the beans are tender; the cooking time will vary depending on the type of bean. Season with pepper.

4 Allow the soup to cool slightly, then transfer 450 ml/16 fl oz to a food processor or blender. Process until smooth then return to the stew.

5 Slice the kale crossways into thin ribbons, keeping the tender leaves separate. Add the thicker leaves and cook gently, uncovered, for 10 minutes. Stir in any remaining kale and continue cooking for 5–10 minutes, until all the greens are tender.

6 Taste and adjust the seasoning, if necessary. Ladle into warmed bowls and serve.

60 GREEN BEANS

All beans contain protein, complex carbohydrates and soluble fibre, but green beans are the seedpods themselves, and therefore contain cleansing insoluble fibre.

In pregnancy, removing toxins from the body before they can do harm becomes even more imperative, because the placenta may not be able to filter out everything that the body is exposed to. Insoluble fibre is particularly good at absorbing toxic matter and excess salts. At the same time, it draws water into stools, regulating digestion, and easing any problems with constipation or diarrhoea. The vitamin C and B vitamins in green beans also support the health of the intestines. Choose green beans to balance the blood sugar and provide slow-release energy. All foods that do this help to regulate weight and appetite, thereby encouraging an expectant mother to put on weight steadily and appropriately by making the right food choices.

- Insoluble fibre removes toxins that may harm the foetus, and regulates bowel function to prevent constipation or diarrhoea.
- Fibre, vitamin C and the B vitamins support digestive health.
- Green beans regulate energy and appetite, encouraging only appropriate weight gain.

Practical tips:

Green beans come in many varieties, including runner beans, French beans and mangetout. All are seedpods with tiny seed forms of the bean inside and can be eaten whole. Steam, boil or add to soups, stews or stir-fries. Green beans are an easy way to add some protein to a simple vegetable dish.

DID YOU KNOW?

Green beans provide a healthy dose of fibre, keeping the body regular when the bowel muscle relaxes and sometimes slows down. The relaxing of muscles is due to the pregnancy hormone relaxin, which allows the womb to stretch.

MAJOR NUTRIENTS PER 100 G/3½ OZ GREEN BEANS

Kcalories	31
Total fat	0.1 g
Protein	1.8 g
Carbohydrate	7.1 g
Fibre	3.6 g
Vitamin C	16 mg
Vitamin B2	0.1 mg
Vitamin B3	0.7 mg
Vitamin B5	0.2 mg
Vitamin B6	0.1 mg
Folate	33 mcg
Choline	15.3 mg

Green bean and potato curry

SERVES 2–4

3 tbsp vegetable oil

1 tsp white cumin seeds

1 tsp mixed mustard and onion
   seeds

3 fresh tomatoes, sliced

1 tsp finely chopped fresh ginger

1 tsp crushed fresh garlic

1 tsp chilli powder

200 g/7 oz green beans, diagonally
   sliced into 2.5-cm/1-inch
   lengths

2 potatoes, peeled and diced

300 ml/10 fl oz water

chopped fresh coriander, to garnish

Method

1 Heat the oil in a large, heavy-based saucepan. Add the white
   cumin seeds and the mustard and onion seeds, stirring well.

2 Add the tomatoes to the pan and stir-fry the mixture for
   3–5 minutes.

3 Mix together the ginger, garlic and chilli powder in a bowl and add
   to the pan. Stir until combined. Add the green beans and potatoes
   to the saucepan and stir-fry for 5 minutes.

4 Add the water to the saucepan, reduce the heat and simmer for
   10–15 minutes, stirring occasionally. Transfer to a warmed serving
   dish, garnish with chopped coriander and serve.

4

Third Trimester

The last months of pregnancy are a period of intense growth. If you are not eating healthily, your own energy and health can suffer because your baby's requirements are so high. However, it is only during this trimester that you actually need more calories; just 10 per cent more, so an extra snack or few slices of bread daily will be sufficient. Ensuring your extra food has high nutritional value is crucial, especially as less room in your stomach means you may need to eat little and often.

Protein needs are high to provide building blocks for your baby's growing body, and foods that supply this and the growth nutrients folate (folic acid), zinc and vitamin C are key. Minerals like magnesium, calcium and potassium support the bone health and heartbeat of both mother and baby.

(G) Growth of baby
(B) Brain development of baby
(A) Immunity-supporting antioxidants
(N) Natural remedy
(V) Suitable for vegetarians
(Q) Quick and easy to prepare

61 ADZUKI BEANS

Adzuki beans contain protein, fibre and carbohydrates. They are also rich in many nutrients that sustain intense growth during this last trimester.

DID YOU KNOW?

Adzuki beans contain both proanthocyanidins and catechins. These antioxidant flavonoids help to ensure the baby's lungs develop correctly, in preparation for his or her first breath.

MAJOR NUTRIENTS PER 100 G/3½ oz ADZUKI BEANS

Kcalories	329
Total fat	0.53 g
Protein	19.87 g
Carbohydrate	62.9 g
Fibre	12.7 g
Vitamin B1	0.45 mg
Vitamin B2	0.22 mg
Vitamin B3	2.63 mg
Vitamin B5	1.47 mg
Vitamin B6	0.35 mg
Folate	622 mcg
Calcium	66 mg
Magnesium	127 mg
Potassium	1,254 mg
Phosphorus	381 mg
Iron	4.98 mg
Zinc	5.04 mg

One of these nutrients is zinc, low levels of which have been shown to result in lower birth weights. With less room available for the mother's stomach, zinc is also important in keeping up appetite, encouraging a little-but-often eating regime of nutrient-dense foods. The folate (folic acid) in adzuki beans is used to make the DNA that facilitates growth as well as the extra red blood cells needed at this stage of pregnancy, when blood volume has increased by 40–50 per cent. The high magnesium and potassium levels in the beans assist this process by enabling the heart muscle to keep circulation flowing to the womb and reduce common third trimester symptoms, such as high blood pressure, puffiness, fatigue and muscle cramps.

- Provide nutrients for growth, energy and detoxification, including zinc, which enables the baby to grow to optimal size.
- Zinc also keeps appetite strong so that both mother and baby can keep up their energy levels.
- Folate supports DNA and red blood cell production for growth.
- Magnesium and potassium keep up the circulation and help prevent high blood pressure, bloating and cramps.

Practical tips:
Adzuki beans can be bought pre-cooked and frozen, and are ideal for slow cooking. Add them cooked to vegetable soups to bulk up the protein content.

Spicy adzuki bean stew

SERVES 2   (G)(A)(V)

100 g/3½ oz dried adzuki beans,
    soaked overnight

2 tbsp vegetable oil

1 large onion, chopped

3 garlic cloves, chopped

1 stick celery, sliced

2 carrots, sliced

4-cm/1½-inch piece fresh ginger,
    peeled and sliced into rounds

1 tsp ground cumin

2 tsp ground coriander

3 cardamom pods, split

300 ml/10 fl oz vegetable stock

100 g/3½ oz baby spinach leaves

pepper

Method

1 Drain and rinse the soaked adzuki beans then transfer to a pan, cover with plenty of water and bring to the boil. Reduce the heat to low, cover the pan, and simmer the beans for 40–50 minutes, until tender, then drain.

2 Meanwhile, heat the oil in a pan and sauté the onion for 6 minutes, until softened. Add the garlic, celery and carrots and cook, stirring, for another 5 minutes. Stir in the spices, add the stock and simmer, part-covered, for 10 minutes. Set aside.

3 When the adzuki beans are tender, drain and transfer them to the pan with the onion mixture. Add the spinach and reheat for 5 minutes, or until wilted. Season with pepper, removing the ginger and cardamom before serving.

62 CHERRIES

Cherries make a superior sweet treat. They taste delicious and, unlike cakes and biscuits, bring balance to your blood sugar, rather than rob you of energy.

At this stage, the baby is producing around 100,000 new brain cells a minute, but these are easily damaged or destroyed by free radicals. Free radicals are unstable molecules that enter the body via pollution and chemicals, cooked foods, electrical equipment and our natural metabolic processes. The proanthocyanidins in cherries, which are demonstrated by the deep red colour of the fruit, are antioxidant bioflavonoids that quench free radicals. Working alongside the vitamin C in the fruit, they also have an anti-inflammatory action, helping prevent pre-eclampsia and skin problems and relieving pain. Antioxidants also support the mother's immunity, which is directly passed on to the baby, helping prevent illness that can take energy away from the vital process of growth.

- Antioxidants destroy harmful toxins to protect the growing baby's brain.
- Proanthocyanidins work with vitamin C to help prevent inflammation and infection in both mother and baby.

Practical tips:
For taste and to get the most vitamin C, cherries are best eaten fresh, with stalks intact. Choose darker colours for more proanthocyanidin content. Think of them as a wonderful treat – both delicious and healthy, if also on the pricey side. A portion of cherries now and then will help keep your bowels regular when they may be sluggish.

DID YOU KNOW?

The antioxidants provided by cherries play a major role in curbing inflammation. They work most effectively when included in a diet high in omega-3 fatty acids, which can be obtained from oily fish, nuts and seeds.

MAJOR NUTRIENTS PER 100 G/3½ OZ CHERRIES

Kcalories	63
Total fat	0 g
Protein	1.06 g
Carbohydrate	16.01 g
Fibre	2.1 g
Vitamin C	7 mg
Potassium	222 mg
Lutein/Zeaxanthin	85 mcg

Cherry sundae

SERVES 2 Ⓖ Ⓑ Ⓐ Ⓥ Ⓠ

150 g/5½ oz strawberries, hulled

1–2 tsp clear honey, to taste

1 tsp vanilla bean paste or extract

200 g/7 oz natural bio yogurt

175 g/6 oz fresh cherries, stoned and halved

40 g/1½ oz hazelnuts, roughly chopped

Method

1 Put the strawberries in a food processor or blender and blend until puréed. Transfer to a bowl then stir in the honey and vanilla bean paste. Lightly stir the strawberry and vanilla sauce into the yogurt.

2 Divide the cherries between 2 tall glasses, before topping with the strawberry yogurt mixture. Scatter over the hazelnuts before serving.

63 PINEAPPLE

At this stage of pregnancy the mother may crave sugar to satisfy the baby's energy requirements. Pineapple is a healthy and nutritious way to deal with these cravings.

In the third trimester, the baby begins to squash the mother's digestive organs and reduce her stomach volume. As the bump grows, higher levels of the hormone relaxin, which relaxes the oesophagus and reduces the efficiency of the digestive muscles, can cause constipation and heartburn. Pineapple helps all the digestive processes and relieves these symptoms. It also contains vitamin C and the mineral manganese, which safeguard the increased production of sex hormones needed to maintain the pregnancy and induce labour at the right time. These nutrients also support blood sugar balance, providing constant energy to both mother and baby. They are necessary, too, for bone development.

- Helps digestive actions, relieving constipation and heartburn.
- Vitamin C and manganese allow the pregnancy sex hormones to rise appropriately and eventually induce labour. They also enable rapid bone development.
- Pineapple helps steady blood sugar balance, providing energy to all cells and for growth.

Practical tips:
In many cultures, pineapple is avoided until the very end of pregnancy because it is believed to soften the cervix and bring on labour. In fact, you would need to eat a huge amount to achieve this effect, which anyway remains unproven. A few slices is nothing to be concerned about, and helps digestion when eaten after a meal.

DID YOU KNOW?
Along with nipple stimulation, sex and curry, eating lots of pineapple is believed to help induce labour when overdue, because the stimulating action of the digestive system encourages contractions.

MAJOR NUTRIENTS PER MEDIUM-SIZED FRESH PINEAPPLE SLICE

Kcalories	40
Total fat	0 g
Protein	0.5 g
Carbohydrate	10.6 g
Fibre	1.2 g
Vitamin C	43 mg
Magnesium	41 mg
Potassium	97 mg
Manganese	148 mg

Sweet and sour fish salad

SERVES 4 Ⓖ Ⓐ Ⓝ Ⓠ

225 g/8 oz trout fillets, rinsed

225 g/8 oz white fish fillets
  (such as line-caught haddock
  or cod)

300 ml/½ pint water

1 stalk lemon grass

2 lime leaves

1 large red chilli

1 bunch spring onions, trimmed
  and shredded

115 g/4 oz fresh pineapple, diced

1 small red pepper, deseeded and
  diced

1 bunch watercress, washed and
  trimmed

fresh snipped chives, to garnish

Dressing

1 tbsp sunflower oil

1 tbsp rice wine vinegar

pinch of chilli powder

1 tsp clear honey

pepper

Method

1 Place the fish in a frying pan and pour over the water. Bend the lemon grass in half to bruise it and add to the pan with the lime leaves. Prick the chilli with a fork and add to the pan. Bring to the boil, reduce the heat and simmer for 7–8 minutes. Let cool.

2 Drain the fish thoroughly, flake the flesh away from the skin and place in a bowl. Gently stir in the spring onions, pineapple and pepper.

3 Arrange the watercress on 4 serving plates and spoon the cooked fish mixture on top.

4 To make the dressing, mix together the first four ingredients and season with a little pepper. Spoon over the fish and serve garnished with snipped chives.

64 PRUNES

Prunes contain the natural laxative dihydrophenylisatin which, together with their fibre content, helps keep a sluggish pregnancy bowel regular.

Prunes offer a much safer and gentler alternative to laxatives, such as senna and cascara. Both the squashing of the digestive organs and colon, and the effect on the muscles of the pregnancy hormone relaxin, can cause a go-slow. This is not only uncomfortable, but can also cause a toxic build-up, while any straining and lower bowel pressure increases the risk of haemorrhoids. The antioxidants vitamin C and rutin in prunes help prevent piles by keeping the veins intact, and therefore also help relieve any tendency to easy bruising and varicose veins. The fibre pectin soaks up toxic metals, such as mercury, aluminium and lead, stopping them reaching the baby. Meanwhile, the carotenoids beta carotene, lutein and zeaxanthin provide antioxidant protection for the baby's brain and eyes.

- Gentle laxative action removes toxins.
- Vitamin C and rutin help prevent haemorrhoids, as well as varicose veins and bruising.
- Fatty antioxidant carotenoids protect the growing baby's brain and eyes.

DID YOU KNOW?

Prunes are dried plums, and their sugar content becomes concentrated during the drying process. They offer an immediate energy source during late pregnancy.

MAJOR NUTRIENTS PER 100 G/3½ OZ PRUNES

Kcalories	240
Total fat	0.38 g
Protein	2.18 g
Carbohydrate	63.88 g
Fibre	7.1 g
Calcium	43 mg
Magnesium	41 mg
Beta carotene	394 mcg
Lutein/Zeaxanthin	148 mcg

Practical tips:
Prunes are extremely satisfying snacks that, although sweet, help regulate blood sugar levels. To relieve constipation, make a prune purée by combining with boiling water in a blender, and add to Bircher muesli or porridge.

Spicy vegetable and prune stew

SERVES 4   (B) (A) (N) (V)

2 tbsp olive oil

1 onion, finely chopped

2–4 garlic cloves, crushed

1 fresh red chilli, deseeded and
sliced

1 aubergine, about 225 g/8 oz, cut
into small chunks

small piece fresh ginger, peeled
and grated

1 tsp ground cumin

1 tsp ground coriander

pinch of saffron threads
or ½ tsp turmeric

1–2 cinnamon sticks

450 g/1 lb butternut squash,
peeled, deseeded and cut into
small chunks

225 g/8 oz sweet potatoes,
cut into small chunks

85 g/3 oz ready-to-eat dried prunes

450–600 ml/16 fl oz–1 pint
vegetable stock

4 tomatoes, chopped

400 g/14 oz canned chickpeas,
drained and rinsed

1 tbsp chopped fresh coriander,
to garnish

Method

1 Heat the oil in a large, heavy-based saucepan with a tight-fitting
lid and cook the onion, garlic, chilli and aubergine, stirring frequently,
for 5–8 minutes, until softened. Add the ginger, cumin, coriander
and saffron and cook, stirring constantly, for 2 minutes. Bruise
the cinnamon.

2 Add the cinnamon, squash, sweet potatoes, prunes, stock and
tomatoes to the saucepan and bring to the boil. Reduce the heat,
cover and simmer, stirring occasionally, for 20 minutes. Add the
chickpeas to the saucepan and cook for a further 10 minutes.
Discard the cinnamon and serve garnished with the fresh coriander.

65 TURKEY

Turkey combines B vitamins and protein for a boost to energy and growth. It also helps to keep up mood, so that you can cope with stress and sleep well.

The vitamin B3 in turkey is particularly skilled at helping the body tissues to use oxygen. A mother's body will prioritize her baby's growth over her own, but it's vital to stay healthy to prepare for birth, post-natal recovery and breastfeeding. Vitamin B6 levels are known to drop dramatically during pregnancy and this can result in skin problems and depression. Turkey contains good levels of all the mood-enhancing B vitamins, as well as the amino acid tryptophan, from which we make serotonin, the sleep and mood brain chemical that helps us stay relaxed and positive. The brown meat in turkey contains higher levels of the energizing nutrient coenzyme Q-10, which provides valuable energy and protection for the baby's heart muscle.

- Vitamin B3 oxygenates both mother's and baby's body tissues, promoting growth and repair.
- B vitamins help maintain good skin and mood.
- Tryptophan makes serotonin to regulate mood and sleep.
- Contains coenzyme Q-10, which keeps energy firing in all cells, including the baby's heart.

Practical tips:
Cravings for sugar generally signify a need for more quality fat and protein in the diet. When suffering from fatigue, a few good-quality slices of turkey – organic if possible – with cucumber or avocado on rye crackers can help.

DID YOU KNOW?

By now, protein requirements will have increased by up to a third compared to pre-pregnancy. Turkey provides a high-quality source, containing all of the amino acids necessary for growth.

MAJOR NUTRIENTS PER 100 G/3½ OZ TURKEY, SKIN REMOVED

Kcalories	111
Total fat	0.65 g
Saturated fat	0.21 g
Monounsaturated fat	0.11 g
Protein	24.6 g
Carbohydrate	0 g
Fibre	0 g
Vitamin B3	6.23 mg
Vitamin B5	0.72 mg
Vitamin B6	0.58 mg
Iron	1.17 mg
Zinc	1.24 mg
Glutamic acid	4.02 g

Turkey and rice salad

SERVES 4 (G) (B) (A)

1 litre/1¾ pints chicken stock

175 g/6 oz mixed long-grain and
   wild rice

2 tbsp olive oil

225 g/8 oz skinless, boneless
   turkey breast, cut into thin strips

225 g/8 oz mangetout

115 g/4 oz oyster mushrooms, torn
   into pieces

55 g/2 oz shelled pistachio nuts,
   finely chopped

2 tbsp chopped fresh coriander

1 tbsp snipped fresh garlic chives

1 tbsp balsamic vinegar

pepper

fresh chives, to garnish

Method

1 Reserve 3 tablespoons of the chicken stock and bring the
   remainder to the boil in a large saucepan. Add the rice and cook
   for 30 minutes, or until tender. Drain and leave to cool slightly.

2 Meanwhile, heat 1 tablespoon of the oil in a preheated wok or frying
   pan. Stir-fry the turkey over a medium heat for 3–4 minutes, or until
   cooked through. Using a slotted spoon, transfer the turkey to a
   dish. Add the mangetout and mushrooms to the wok and stir-fry for
   1 minute. Add the reserved stock, bring to the boil, then reduce the
   heat, cover and simmer for 3–4 minutes. Transfer the vegetables to
   the dish and leave to cool slightly.

3 Thoroughly mix the rice, turkey, mangetout, mushrooms, nuts,
   coriander and garlic chives together, then season to taste with
   pepper. Drizzle with the remaining oil and the vinegar and garnish
   with fresh chives. Serve warm.

66 LEEKS

Leeks have a well-deserved reputation as a gentle natural laxative and detoxifying agent, which makes them a perfect choice at a time when the bowel may be slow.

All members of the illustrious allium plant family – leeks, onions and garlic – have a high sulphur content, which helps the liver detoxify harmful substances. This mineral also moves waste products out of individual cells, allowing nutrients to enter. Leeks have high levels of prebiotic fibres, such as inulin, which feed the probiotic beneficial bacteria in your intestines and keep your bowels moving. These prebiotics help you fight infection and encourage good immune responses throughout the body, and convert the plant foods that you eat into energy. All of these actions are important in helping to keep harmful toxins away from the baby. The antibodies that a mother's immune system produces against fungal, viral or bacterial invaders are passed to the foetus through the placenta.

- High sulphur content detoxifies the body and allows nutrients into cells that protect and nourish the baby.
- Prebiotic fibre inulin feeds good digestive bacteria to prevent constipation that can cause toxic build-up.
- Prebiotics also support immunity against invading bacteria and viruses, which is passed on to the baby.

Practical tips:
Leeks can be used in any recipe in place of onion, which may exacerbate heartburn tendencies in the third trimester. Be careful not to overcook leeks because they easily become soggy and lose their flavour. Use them as a base for a vegetable broth or soup.

DID YOU KNOW?

Leeks, along with onions, garlic, spinach, parsley and carrots, contain the substance sulfoquinovosyl diacylglycerol, which is known to stop cancer cells growing and may help prevent the risk of childhood cancers in the unborn baby.

MAJOR NUTRIENTS PER MEDIUM-SIZED LEEK

Kcalories	54
Total fat	0.27 g
Protein	1.33 g
Carbohydrate	12.59 g
Fibre	1.6 g
Vitamin C	10.7 mg
Vitamin B6	0.21 mg
Vitamin K	41.8 mcg
Folate	57 mcg
Calcium	53 mg
Magnesium	25 mg

Leek and herb soufflés

SERVES 4 (B) (A) (V)

1 tbsp olive oil
350 g/12 oz baby leeks,
    finely chopped
125 ml/4 fl oz vegetable stock
50 g/1¾ oz walnuts
2 eggs, separated
2 tbsp chopped mixed herbs
2 tbsp natural bio yogurt
butter, for greasing
pepper

Method

1 Preheat the oven to 180°C/350°F/Gas Mark 4. Heat the olive oil in a frying pan. Add the leeks and sauté over a medium heat, stirring occasionally, for 2–3 minutes.

2 Add the vegetable stock to the pan, reduce the heat and simmer gently for a further 5 minutes.

3 Place the walnuts in a food processor or blender and process until finely chopped. Add the leek mixture to the nuts and process briefly to form a purée. Transfer to a mixing bowl.

4 Mix together the egg yolks, the herbs and the yogurt until thoroughly combined. Pour the egg mixture into the leek purée. Season with pepper to taste and mix well.

5 In a separate, grease-free mixing bowl, whisk the egg whites until firm peaks form.

6 Fold the egg whites into the leek mixture. Spoon the mixture into four 150-ml/5-fl oz ovenproof ramekins, lightly greased with butter and place on a warmed baking tray.

7 Cook in the preheated oven for 35–40 minutes, or until well risen and set. Serve the soufflés immediately.

67

RASPBERRY LEAF TEA

Raspberry leaf tea, which is thought to ease birth pain and complication, has a long-standing tradition as a herbal support during the third trimester.

Raspberry leaf tea contains an alkaloid called fragine that helps tone and strengthen the uterine and pelvic muscles. This effect may help shorten the second stage of labour. More effective muscle contractions can help reduce pain because the muscles remain oxygenated and don't build up lactic acid through stress. Some studies have shown that these effects may result in less complication and intervention during labour: specifically, fewer Caesarean and forceps deliveries in those women who had regularly drunk it in their third trimester. In one study, two-thirds of midwives recommended raspberry leaf tea as a known remedy to help women. The tea's rich and varied mineral content is also believed to help birth.

- Fragine tones muscles in the womb and pelvis to make contractions stronger during labour.
- May help shorten the second stage of labour, reduce labour pains and reduce the likelihood of intervention.
- Its rich mineral content, although not quantified, is believed to aid muscle contractions.

Practical tips:
Due to its effects on the uterus, many sources recommend waiting until week 36 of pregnancy before drinking raspberry leaf tea. If the pregnancy has had any serious complications, consult your healthcare provider first. Drink 1–2 cups per day of the fresh leaf infusion or, if using teabags, 2–3 cups.

DID YOU KNOW?

The alkaloids in raspberry leaf tea that prepare the uterus for labour may also help to shrink it back to normal size after birth, as well as encourage the production of breast milk.

MAJOR NUTRIENTS PER 225 ML/8 FL OZ RASPBERRY TEA

Kcalories - approx*	2
Total fat	0 g

* No other data available – it is not researched/quantified

Raspberry leaf punch

SERVES 2 (A)(N)(V)(Q)

1 raspberry leaf tea bag
300 ml/10 fl oz just-boiled water
200 ml/7 fl oz raspberry juice
100 ml/3½ fl oz orange juice
½ apple, cored and sliced into
  half moons
6 slices cucumber, halved
few mint leaves
ice cubes, to serve (optional)

Method

1 Prepare a cup of raspberry leaf tea using the water. Leave to cool and remove the tea bag.
2 Pour the cooled raspberry leaf tea into a jug with the raspberry and orange juices, apple slices, cucumber and mint leaves. Serve chilled with ice cubes, if using.

68 WATERCRESS

Watercress is a fantastically easy way to add cleansing sulphur, protective antioxidants and energy-giving chlorophyll to the pregnancy diet.

MAJOR NUTRIENTS PER 25 G/1 OZ WATERCRESS

Kcalories	3
Total fat	0 g
Protein	0.6 g
Carbohydrate	0.3 g
Fibre	0.1 g
Vitamin C	11 mg
Vitamin A	798 IU
Vitamin E	0.25 mg
Folate	2.25 mcg
Beta carotene	478 mcg
Lutein/Zeaxanthin	1,442 mcg

Watercress contains the sulphur compounds isothiocyanates. These are very efficient at helping the liver escort out harmful toxins that might otherwise harm the baby. Sulphur helps deliver nutrients and oxygen around the body, aiding its ability to work with vitamin C to produce the collagen that forms the baby's skeleton, muscle and skin. With vitamins A and E, they enable the mother's skin to stretch while causing minimal damage, and may reduce the baby's future risk of eczema and asthma. The dark green of watercress leaves signifies high levels of the antioxidant carotenoids, beta carotene and lutein, that strengthen both mother's and baby's immune system and vision.

• Sulphur eliminates harmful toxins and aids circulation so that oxygen and nutrients can be delivered to the baby.
• Sulphur and vitamins A, C and E help create the baby's bone, skin and muscle and the mother's expanding skin.
• May help prevent the baby developing eczema and asthma.
• Carotenoids beta carotene and lutein strengthen both mother's and baby's immune systems and vision.

Practical tips:
The darkest green leaves have the most carotenoids and the energizing plant pigment chlorophyll. Choose fresh, open bunches rather than those in sealed bags. Add watercress to meals as you would any salad leaf. The bitter taste stimulates digestion.

Chilli squid with watercress

SERVES 4   (G) (A) (Q)

12 squid tubes and tentacles
(about 700 g/1 lb 9 oz total
weight), cleaned and prepared
2–3 tbsp olive oil
1–2 red chillies, deseeded
and thinly sliced
2 spring onions, finely chopped
lemon wedges, for squeezing,
plus extra to serve
3 good handfuls watercress
2 handfuls baby spinach or rocket
pepper

Dressing
100 ml/3½ fl oz olive oil
juice of 1 lime
2 shallots, thinly sliced
1 tomato, peeled, deseeded
and finely chopped
1 garlic clove, crushed
pepper

Method

1 To make the dressing, mix together all the ingredients in a bowl,
season with pepper to taste, cover and refrigerate until required.

2 Cut the squid tubes into 5-cm/2-inch pieces, then score diamond
patterns lightly across the flesh with the tip of a sharp knife. Heat
the oil in a wok or large frying pan over a high heat, add the squid
pieces and tentacles and stir-fry for 1 minute. Add the chillies and
spring onions and stir-fry for a further minute. Season to taste with
pepper and add a good squeeze of lemon juice.

3 Mix the watercress and spinach together, then toss with enough
of the dressing to coat lightly. Serve immediately with the squid,
together with lemon wedges to squeeze over the squid.

69

COCONUT WATER

Coconut water is a natural isotonic, with the same electrolyte mineral content as blood plasma. It will naturally hydrate and support the body's higher blood volume.

The electrolyte minerals calcium, magnesium, sodium and potassium in coconut water are essential to health because they govern electrical impulses and fluid balances in our bodies. They also support the heart as it works 25 per cent harder than usual to pump the extra blood. The baby uses up these minerals for the benefit of its own nervous system and fluids, so if the mother does not replenish stocks, she may suffer deficiency symptoms arising from dehydration, such as muscle cramps, puffiness, fatigue or headaches. Coconut water is also a good source of energy. The lauric acid it contains destroys bacteria and viruses, and is also found in human breast milk.

- The 40–50 per cent increase in blood volume at this time demands higher levels of electrolyte minerals.
- Mother's and baby's muscles, heart and brain rely on this extra level of hydration and energy.
- Helps prevent electrolyte mineral deficiencies, such as muscle cramps and fatigue.
- Lauric acid protects against viruses and bacteria.

Practical tips:
Coconut water can be siphoned from young, green coconuts. It is also available in cartons. Drink it daily in the run up to the due date to keep the muscles supplied with the minerals it needs for efficient contractions. Coconut water is an ideal energy drink during labour.

DID YOU KNOW?

The sodium in coconut water is an essential mineral but because modern diets can be too high in sodium chloride or table salt, it can get out of balance with potassium, commonly low. Here the two minerals are in the right balance to nourish the baby's kidneys and muscles.

MAJOR NUTRIENTS PER 225 ML/8 FL OZ COCONUT WATER

Kcalories	46
Total fat	0.48 g
Lauric acid	211 mg
Protein	1.73 g
Carbohydrate	8.9 g
Fibre	2.6 g
Vitamin C	5.8 mg
Calcium	58 mg
Magnesium	60 mg
Potassium	600 mg
Sodium	252 mg

Fresh coconut juice

SERVES 2 Ⓑ Ⓐ Ⓝ Ⓥ Ⓠ

2 apples, quartered and cored
1 stick celery, trimmed
8-cm/3½-inch piece cucumber,
   quartered lengthways
200 ml/7fl oz coconut water

Method

1 Put the apples, celery and cucumber in a food processor or blender and process until smooth. Pour into a jug then add the coconut water and stir until combined. Serve immediately.

70

BUTTER

Butter provides many components that are crucial to growth, reproduction and health. It can support increased energy and hormone needs during pregnancy.

There has been a lot of negative press about saturated fats over the past 20 years, but many scientists now believe that they are part of our natural diet and create an important balance with dietary omega-3 and omega-6 fatty acids. Butter provides lecithin, which helps break down fats for absorption so that the baby can use them to make cells. What's more, the sex hormones oestrogen and progesterone, produced in very high amounts in the third trimester, can only be made from fats. The butyric acid, myristic acid and lauric acid in butter are MCTs (Medium-Chain Triglycerides) that fuel your gut cells to keep in check your defence against bacteria and viruses. We can't store these fats, but use them as dense sources of energy. Lauric acid is also found in human breast milk, a densely fatty substance that the body is now preparing to make.

- Lecithin helps a mother digest crucial fats that can be incorporated into the baby's growing body.
- MCTs support the immune system and digestive function, and can be passed on to the baby.
- Lauric acid and other fats in butter provide the building materials for breast milk.

Practical tips:
Fatigue in pregnancy can occur if there are not enough quality fats in the diet. Butter from grass-fed cows also contains CLA (conjugated linoleic acid), which helps regulate weight.

DID YOU KNOW?
Research has shown that native peoples with diets higher in animal fats from meat have healthier levels of the fat-soluble nutrients such as the vitamins A, D and E found in butter, which protect an unborn baby, than vegetarian tribes.

MAJOR NUTRIENTS PER 25 G/1 oz BUTTER

Kcalories	215
Total fat	24.33 g
Monounsaturated fat	6.31 g
Saturated fat	15.4 g
Butyric acid	968 mg
Lauric acid	776 mg
Myristic acid	2,231 mg
Protein	0.26 g
Carbohydrate	0.02 g
Fibre	0 g
Vitamin A	750 IU
Vitamin E	0.7 mg
Vitamin D	18 IU

Grilled halibut with garlic butter

SERVES 4 (G)(B)(A)(Q)

6 tbsp butter, plus extra
*   for greasing*
4 halibut fillets, about 175 g/6 oz
*   each, rinsed and patted dry*
2 garlic cloves, finely chopped
pepper
sprigs of fresh flat-leaf parsley,
*   to garnish*
cooked French beans and lime
*   wedges, to serve*

Method

1 Preheat the grill to medium. Grease a shallow, heatproof dish with
   butter, then arrange the fish in it. Season with pepper.
2 In a separate bowl, mix the butter with the garlic. Arrange pieces of
   the garlic butter all over the fish, then transfer to the grill. Cook for
   7–8 minutes, turning once, until the fish is cooked through.
3 Remove the dish from the grill. Using a fish slice, remove the fillets
   from the dish and arrange on individual serving plates. Pour over the
   remaining melted butter from the dish, and garnish with the parsley
   sprigs. Serve with the French beans and lime wedges.

71 PEAS

Peas are a nutritionally dense convenience food. The fibre, zinc and B vitamins help regulate blood sugar levels to sustain energy in mother and baby.

Iron also supports your energy levels, by producing energy in the cells and within muscles, both of which are vital for the baby's rapidly growing body. Dietary protein from plant, as well as animal sources, maintains your body's acid:alkaline balance. A balanced pH ensures that the immune, hormonal and detoxification systems work optimally and that the kidneys don't become overloaded at a time when they are under pressure from increased blood volume. An increased availability of calcium, which peas can provide, may reduce the body's response to pain during childbirth. Low levels of calcium have been linked to premature births, because tense muscles can cause early uterine contractions.

- Fibre, zinc, iron and the B vitamins enable constant energy generation to support the baby's growing body.
- Protein helps the body systems work efficiently. The kidneys in particular need support because they are dealing with more fluid.
- Contain calcium, which is thought to play a role in regulating pain in labour through decreased nerve responses; tense muscles resulting from calcium deficiency may lead to early labour.

Practical tips:
Always keep a packet of peas in the freezer, so that even when you are tired or can't face preparing vegetables you can add some greenery to your plate. A simple bowl of peas makes a light meal or snack in itself. Add a knob of butter and some pepper to taste.

DID YOU KNOW?

Peas are a legume (bean) rather than a vegetable, which means they are high in protein. They cause less gas in women who find other beans, such as lentils, difficult to digest during pregnancy.

MAJOR NUTRIENTS PER 100 G/3½ OZ PEAS

Kcalories	81
Total fat	0.4 g
Protein	5.4 g
Carbohydrate	14.5 g
Fibre	5.1 g
Vitamin C	40 mg
Vitamin B3	2.1 mg
Folate	65 mcg
Calcium	56 mg
Magnesium	33 mg
Potassium	244 mg
Iron	1.5 mg
Zinc	1.2 mg
Lutein/Zeaxanthin	2,477 mcg

Minty pea and bean soup

SERVES 4–6   (G) (A)

1½ tbsp olive oil

1 bunch spring onions, trimmed
   and chopped

1 large celery stick, chopped

1 garlic clove, crushed

1 floury potato, about 150 g/5½ oz,
   peeled and diced

1.2 litres/2 pints vegetable stock

1 bay leaf

150 g/5½ oz peas

400 g/14 oz canned flageolet
   beans, drained and rinsed

pepper

finely shredded fresh mint,
   to garnish

mixed-grain bread rolls, to serve

Method

1 Heat the oil in a large saucepan over a medium–high heat. Add the
   spring onions, celery and garlic and cook, stirring, for about
   3 minutes, until soft. Add the potato and stir for a further minute.

2 Add the stock, bay leaf and pepper to taste and bring to the boil,
   stirring. Reduce the heat to low, cover the pan and simmer for
   20 minutes, or until the potatoes are tender. Add the peas and
   beans and return the soup to the boil.

3 Reduce the heat, cover, and continue to simmer until the peas are
   tender. Remove the bay leaf, then tip the soup into a food processor
   or blender and blend until smooth. Place a metal sieve over the
   rinsed-out pan and use a wooden spoon to push the soup through
   the sieve.

4 Add pepper to taste and reheat. Ladle the soup into warmed soup
   bowls, sprinkle with mint and serve with the bread rolls.

72

GARLIC

Garlic has a long history of use as an anti-fungal. The regular inclusion of garlic in the diet keeps a check on yeast organisms that can cause thrush.

Vaginal thrush becomes more likely in late pregnancy as oestrogen levels reach their peak. This risk is increased if the mother's diet includes lots of refined sugars. The allicin in garlic is a strong alternative to antifungal medications that can affect beneficial bacteria levels and therefore both mother's and baby's immunity. Vaginal thrush can also be passed to the baby during birth or afterwards through breastfeeding, causing oral thrush and nappy rash. The potent antioxidants and sulphur compounds in garlic also remove toxins and may help reduce problems with nasal congestion and breathing that are common in the third trimester. The prebiotic fibre inulin fuels beneficial bacteria, reducing the severity of fungal, bacterial and viral infections and the likelihood of inflammation and intolerances.

- Antifungal action that doesn't upset natural beneficial bacteria levels and helps stop a mother passing thrush to the baby.
- Antioxidants and sulphur compounds support immune function and eliminate harmful toxins.
- Prebiotic fibre supports healthy probiotic bacteria levels so that the body can ward off infection.

Practical tips:
Eat garlic raw where possible to obtain its full potency. Garlic needs to be chopped, crushed or chewed to release the allicin. Add crushed garlic to olive oil for a simple salad dressing.

DID YOU KNOW?
Recent research has found that when garlic was added to the placenta cells of women who either experienced pre-eclampsia or delivered a baby with a low birth weight, the quality of those cells improved because the enzymes that contribute to both these problems were eliminated.

MAJOR NUTRIENTS PER 2 CLOVES RAW GARLIC

Kcalories	8
Total fat	0.2 g
Protein	0.38 g
Carbohydrate	0.99 g
Fibre	0.2 g
Vitamin C	0.9 mg

Lemon and garlic spinach

SERVES 4   (A)(N)(V)(Q)

4 tbsp olive oil
2 garlic cloves, thinly sliced
450 g/1 lb fresh spinach,
    torn or shredded
juice of ½ lemon
pepper

Method

1 Heat the olive oil over a high heat in a large frying pan. Add the garlic and spinach and cook, stirring constantly, until the spinach is soft. Take care not to let the spinach burn.

2 Remove from the heat, turn into a serving bowl and sprinkle with lemon juice. Season with a little pepper. Mix well and serve either hot or at room temperature.

73 SALMON

Salmon provides protein and antioxidants in support of growth, and the omega-3 fatty acids that are necessary for the health of the joints, eyes and brain.

Although plant foods such as walnuts contain omega-3 fatty acids, our bodies need to convert these before DHA and EPA can be produced. It is easier for the body to obtain the DHA and EPA directly from oily fish, such as salmon. DHA is then immediately incorporated into the hundreds of thousands of new brain and nervous-system cells that the baby is producing by the minute. One study found that women with higher DHA levels had babies that were two months ahead developmentally in the first six months of life, though other studies have found no clear link. Vitamins A and D and the B vitamins also support brain function and cognition, including the mother's mood before and after birth. The EPA in salmon supports heart function and makes the substance resolvin that prevents inflammation, which can be a problem in the joints as the body becomes heavier.

- A direct source of the omega-3 fatty acids DHA and EPA.
- DHA supports intense brain growth.
- Vitamins A and D and the B vitamins help support the mother's mood as well as the baby's brain function.
- EPA supports heart function and helps joints stay pain-free.

Practical tips:
Wild salmon has higher levels of omega-3 fatty acids than farmed. These fatty acids can be damaged, so don't overcook – lightly poach or steam and ensure it is cooked right through but is not dry.

DID YOU KNOW?

The DHA and EPA requirements of the baby's brain are so high at this point that if oily fish is absent from the diet, it is advisable to take a fish oil or vegan marine algae DHA supplement.

MAJOR NUTRIENTS PER 100 G/3½ OZ WILD SALMON

Kcalories	142
Total fat	6.34 g
Omega-3 fatty acids – DHA	1.12 g
Omega-3 fatty acids – EPA	0.32 g
Protein	19.9 g
Carbohydrate	0 g
Fibre	0 g
Vitamin B3	7.9 mg
Vitamin B5	1.64 mg
Vitamin B6	0.81 mg
Vitamin B12	2.8 mcg
Vitamin A	40 IU
Vitamin D	435 IU
Choline	94.6 mg
Calcium	12 mg
Magnesium	29 mg
Potassium	490 mg
Phosphorus	200 mg
Selenium	36.5 mcg

Warm salmon and mango salad

SERVES 4 (G) (B) (A)

115 g/4 oz yellow or red
  cherry tomatoes
2–3 salmon fillets, about
  150 g/5½ oz each, skinned
  and cut into small cubes
1 large ripe mango (about
  150 g/ 5½ oz prepared fruit),
  peeled and cut into
  small chunks
2 tbsp orange juice
1 tbsp soy sauce
115 g/4 oz mixed salad leaves
½ cucumber, trimmed and sliced
  into batons
6 spring onions, trimmed
  and chopped

Dressing
4 tbsp natural yogurt
1 tsp soy sauce
1 tbsp finely grated orange rind

Method

1 Cut half of the tomatoes in
  half and set aside. Thread
  the salmon, with the whole
  tomatoes and half of the
  mango chunks, onto 4 pre-
  soaked wooden skewers.
  Mix the orange juice and soy
  sauce together in a small bowl
  and brush over the kebabs.
  Leave to marinate for 15
  minutes, brushing with the
  remaining orange juice mixture
  at least once more.

2 Arrange the salad leaves
  on a serving platter with the
  remaining halved tomatoes,
  mango chunks, cucumber
  and spring onions.

3 To make the dressing, mix
  together the yogurt, soy sauce
  and grated orange rind in a
  small bowl and reserve.

4 Preheat the grill to high and
  line the grill rack with foil.
  Place the salmon kebabs on
  the grill rack, brush again with
  the marinade and grill for 5–7
  minutes, or until the salmon
  is cooked. Turn the kebabs
  over halfway through cooking
  and brush with any remaining
  marinade.

5 Divide the prepared salad
  between 4 plates, top each
  with a kebab, and then drizzle
  with the dressing.

74 RED PEPPERS

Red peppers are one of the richest sources of vitamin C. Vitamin C is the most abundant micronutrient in the body, and the need for it increases during pregnancy.

This is particularly true in the third trimester when vitamin C is used up quickly to help produce the sex hormones oestrogen and progesterone that maintain pregnancy and prepare the body for birth and breastfeeding. Vitamin C is naturally purged from the body via the urine about twice a day, so it is difficult to have too much of it, and our need is constant. It also supports the collagen production of the baby's rapidly growing body that is necessary for all its structures, including skin, bone, teeth and muscle. Vitamin C allows calcium in the diet to be absorbed to make the baby's skeleton and to keep the mother's own bones and teeth from suffering. It also allows iron to be absorbed and is used to keep blood oxygenated. The vitamin B6 and folate (folic acid) in red peppers support healthy brain function and detoxification processes.

- Vitamin C maintains healthy levels of the hormones needed to sustain pregnancy and enable birth and breastfeeding.
- Vitamin C is needed in large amounts for the growth of the baby.
- The absorption of calcium from food relies on vitamin C, as does our utilization of iron for energy.
- Vitamin B6 and folate keep both brain and body free of toxins.

Practical tips:

Choose deep red colours to benefit from the fat-protective antioxidant lycopene. Buy with the green stem intact and cut this at the last minute to preserve the vitamin C content.

DID YOU KNOW?

As our primary antioxidant, vitamin C is concentrated in our organs at levels of 10–100 times greater than in the blood. Sufficient levels are vital for the protection of the baby's own organs, including the heart, liver, lungs and kidneys.

MAJOR NUTRIENTS PER MEDIUM-SIZED RED PEPPER

Kcalories	37
Total fat	0.36 g
Protein	1.18 g
Carbohydrate	7.18 g
Fibre	2.5 g
Vitamin C	152 mg
Vitamin B6	0.35 mg
Folate	55 mcg

Tomato, lentil and red pepper soup

SERVES 4 Ⓖ Ⓐ Ⓥ

3 tbsp olive oil

2 onions, chopped

2 garlic cloves, chopped

2 large red peppers, deseeded and chopped

500 g/1 lb 2 oz ripe tomatoes, chopped

100 g/3½ oz red split lentils

600 ml/1 pint vegetable stock, plus extra to thin (optional)

1 tbsp red wine vinegar

pepper

2 spring onions, chopped, or 1 tbsp snipped fresh chives, to garnish

Method

1 Heat the oil in a large saucepan over a medium–high heat, add the onions and cook, stirring, for 5 minutes, or until softened but not browned. Add the garlic and red peppers and cook, stirring, for 5 minutes, or until the red peppers are softened.

2 Add the tomatoes, lentils and stock and bring to a simmer. Reduce the heat to low, cover and simmer gently for 25 minutes, or until the lentils are tender. Stir in the vinegar and season with pepper to taste.

3 Leave to cool slightly, then transfer the soup to a blender or food processor and blend for 1 minute, or until smooth. Return to the pan and reheat, stirring in a little hot water or stock if the soup seems a little too thick. Serve in warmed soup bowls, garnished with the spring onions.

75 ASPARAGUS

Asparagus offers a wealth of supporting nutrients at this demanding stage of pregnancy, when the need for nutrient-dense foods is at its peak.

Asparagus helps provide the nutrients that work together most efficiently in support of the growing baby and the mother's preparation for birth and breastfeeding. Its rich antioxidant profile, which includes vitamins A and E, the minerals selenium and zinc, the carotenoids lutein and beta carotene and the flavonoids rutin, quercetin and kaempferol, protect DNA and maintain both mother's and baby's immune systems. Added to these and enhancing their action is the antioxidant enzyme glutathione. Asparagus is one of a few foods, including onions, garlic, leeks and bananas, that provide the prebiotic fibre inulin. This fibre enables beneficial gut bacteria to protect mother and baby from infection. With its antioxidants and B vitamins, asparagus also helps remove toxins.

- Antioxidant combinations maintain mother's and baby's immune systems and protect DNA.
- The prebiotic fibre inulin supports internal good bacteria, keeping out invaders that may cause infection.
- Antioxidants and the B vitamins enhance the body's ability to tackle harmful toxic build-up that may harm the baby.

Practical tips:
Asparagus can be eaten hot or cold, in salads, stir-fries, as a side dish or as a starter. It works particularly well with lemon or butter or a few Parmesan shavings. Steaming it will retain the most nutrients. The thicker, woodier large stalks contain the most fibre.

DID YOU KNOW?

Asparagus contains vitamin K, which helps both mother's and baby's natural clotting mechanisms, reducing the risk of internal bleeding after delivery.

MAJOR NUTRIENTS PER 10 ASPARAGUS SPEARS

Kcalories	24
Total fat	0.1 g
Protein	2.64 g
Carbohydrate	4.66 g
Fibre	2.5 g
Vitamin B3	1.17 mg
Vitamin B5	0.33 mg
Vitamin B6	0.11 mg
Vitamin E	1.36 mg
Vitamin A	907 IU
Vitamin K	49.9 mcg
Calcium	29 mg
Magnesium	17 mg
Potassium	242 mg
Zinc	0.65 mg
Selenium	2.8 mcg
Beta carotene	539 mcg
Lutein/Zeaxanthin	852 mcg

Crispy roast asparagus

SERVES 4   (A)(V)(Q)

450 g/1 lb asparagus spears,
   trimmed
2 tbsp extra virgin olive oil
1 tbsp grated Parmesan cheese,
   to serve

Method

1 Preheat the oven to 200°C/400°F/Gas Mark 6.

2 Arrange the asparagus in a single layer on a metal baking sheet. Drizzle with olive oil.

3 Place the tray in the oven and bake for 10–15 minutes, turning once. Remove from the oven, transfer to a dish and serve immediately, sprinkled with the grated Parmesan.

76 POTATOES

Potatoes can help satisfy the daily need for 200–300 extra calories in this trimester. A meal that includes potatoes can also stop you craving dessert afterwards.

Stress, anxiety and sleeplessness are common third trimester problems, when the birth is imminent and activity is harder. Potatoes raise serotonin levels in the brain and this sleep and mood neurotransmitter (brain chemical) promotes relaxation and quality sleep. The vitamin B6 and C in potatoes aids this action and also ensures that energy is released from food at the right times, making it easier to cope with the day. Vitamin B6 is a very important pregnancy nutrient: it makes possible the use of iron, it breaks down and makes use of protein for growth, it draws energy from carbohydrate foods, and it regulates the pregnancy hormones. The vitamin C in potato protects the baby's vulnerable brain and nerve cells as they rapidly develop.

- Potatoes are naturally calming, promoting sleep.
- Vitamin B6 and C help release energy from food and produce serotonin to regulate mood and sleep.
- Vitamin B6 plays an important role in hormonal, growth and energy processes in pregnancy.
- Vitamin C protects the baby's sensitive brain cells.

Practical tips:
Choose new potatoes in their skins to get the most fibre and to benefit from the nutrients that are concentrated under the skin. Older potatoes are far more sugary and have a less positive effect on energy and mood.

DID YOU KNOW?

Chemicals called kukoamines in potatoes work with the vitamin C, B6 and potassium also present to help lower blood pressure, a vital task at a time of increased blood volume and physical stress.

MAJOR NUTRIENTS PER 100 G/3½ OZ POTATOES

Kcalories	77
Total fat	0.1 g
Protein	2 g
Carbohydrate	19 g
Fibre	2.2 g
Vitamin C	20 mg
Vitamin B6	0.25 mg
Potassium	421 mg

Potato and tomato tortilla

SERVES 6   (G) (B) (A) (V) (Q)

1 kg/2 lb 4 oz potatoes, peeled and
   cut into small cubes
2 tbsp olive oil
1 bunch spring onions, chopped
115 g/4 oz cherry tomatoes
6 eggs
3 tbsp water
2 tbsp fresh chopped parsley
pepper

Method

1 Boil the potatoes for 8–10 minutes, or until tender. Drain and reserve
  until required.

2 Heat the oil in a large ovenproof frying pan. Add the spring onions
  and fry until just soft. Add the potatoes and fry for 3–4 minutes,
  until coated with oil and hot. Smooth the top and scatter over the
  tomatoes.

3 Mix the eggs, water, pepper and parsley together in a bowl, then
  pour into the frying pan. Cook over a very gentle heat for 10–15
  minutes, until the tortilla looks fairly set.

4 Preheat the grill to medium. Place the frying pan under the hot grill
  and cook until the top is brown and set. Leave to cool for 10–15
  minutes before sliding out of the frying pan onto a chopping board.
  Cut into wedges and serve immediately.

77

CASHEWS

Cashews are often overlooked in favour of other nuts, but they have excellent levels of the same heart-protective monounsaturated fats found in olive oil.

MAJOR NUTRIENTS PER 25 G/1 OZ CASHEWS

Kcalories	166
Total fat	13.15 g
Monounsaturated fat	7.14 g
Saturated fat	2.34 g
Omega-6 fatty acids	2,335 mg
Protein	5.47 g
Carbohydrate	9.06 g
Fibre	1 g
Vitamin B3	0.32 mg
Vitamin B5	0.26 mg
Vitamin B6	0.125 mg
Calcium	11 mg
Magnesium	88 mg
Potassium	198 mg
Phosphorus	178 mg
Iron	2.0 mg
Zinc	1.73 mg
Manganese	0.50 mg

At this stage, the mother's heart is working 25 per cent harder than usual to pump the extra blood around the body, while the baby's heart is just starting its life, so both need a lot of nutritional support. Studies have shown that the monounsaturated fat, oleic acid, enables the heart to use oxygen and fuel more efficiently. The minerals calcium, magnesium and potassium in cashews also encourage two strong heartbeats, while the B vitamins ensure energy is released fully into every cell. These minerals also regulate nerve and muscle function. One molecule of calcium is needed for every muscle contraction during labour and magnesium helps strengthen muscles in the uterus. These two 'calming minerals' also help relieve stress, and promote relaxation and sleep.

- Oleic acid protects mother's and baby's hearts and allows them to work effectively.
- Calcium, magnesium, potassium and the B vitamins keep heartbeats strong.
- Calcium and magnesium keep the nervous system calm and prepare the muscles for birth contractions.

Practical tips:
Cashews make excellent nut butter, simply blended on their own. If used in cooking, they should only be added at the very end to avoid damaging the omega-6 fatty acids. For this reason, choose raw cashews to snack on rather than roasted.

Cashew nut paella

SERVES 4 (G)(B)(A)(V)

2 tbsp olive oil

1 tbsp butter

1 red onion, chopped

150 g/5½ oz arborio rice

1 tsp turmeric

1 tsp ground cumin

3 garlic cloves, crushed

1 red pepper, deseeded and diced
    (optional)

85 g/3 oz baby corn, halved
    lengthways

2 tbsp stoned black olives

1 large tomato, deseeded
    and diced

450 ml/16 fl oz vegetable stock

85 g/3 oz unsalted cashew nuts

55 g/2 oz frozen peas

2 tbsp chopped fresh flat leaf
    parsley, plus extra to garnish

pinch of cayenne pepper

pepper

Method

1 Heat the olive oil and butter in a large frying pan or paella pan until
   the butter has melted.

2 Add the onion and cook over a medium heat, stirring constantly,
   for 2–3 minutes until softened.

3 Stir in the rice, turmeric, cumin, garlic, red pepper, if using, baby
   corn, olives and tomato and cook over a medium heat, stirring
   occasionally, for 1–2 minutes.

4 Pour in the stock and bring the mixture to the boil. Reduce the heat
   and cook gently, stirring constantly, for a further 20 minutes.

5 Add the cashew nuts and peas and continue to cook, stirring
   occasionally, for a further 5 minutes. Season to taste with pepper
   and add the parsley and a pinch of cayenne pepper. Transfer the
   paella to warm serving plates, and garnish with extra parsley.

78

BUTTERNUT SQUASH

Butternut squash is an energy-supporting vegetable that also contains a wide range of antioxidants to help reduce inflammation, pain, infection and cell damage.

Taking on board high levels of antioxidants from a range of foods, including squash, ensures that the damage to your body caused by elements such as pollution, chemicals, medications and sunlight is limited. The effects can be heightened in the third trimester when added exertion raises stress levels. The vitamins A and C in squash support the fatty and watery parts of the body respectively, and ensure the health of your mucous membranes, helping to relieve any nasal congestion and breathing issues. Protecting these membranes also helps both mother and baby fight infection. The trace mineral manganese in squash provides additional protection from illness by helping to produce the antioxidant enzyme superoxide dismutase (SOD). Manganese also helps the body absorb calcium and create new bone and cartilage.

- Contains antioxidants that protect both mother and baby from environmental and internal stress factors.
- Vitamins A and C support the mucous membranes to reduce nasal problems and fight infection.
- Manganese produces the antioxidant enzyme SOD and supports healthy bone and cartilage growth.

Practical tips:
Use butternut squash as you would any root vegetable. Or simply cut in half, drizzle with olive oil and roast. Butternut squash soup is an easily digested energy source.

DID YOU KNOW?

Calcium and magnesium are needed in a ratio of around 3:2 for both to work in the body. We tend to get more calcium than magnesium in our diets, via dairy foods and water, but squash offers a good balance of the two.

MAJOR NUTRIENTS PER 100 G/3½ OZ SQUASH

Kcalories	45
Total fat	0.1 g
Protein	1 g
Carbohydrate	11.69 g
Fibre	2 g
Vitamin C	21 mg
Vitamin A	10,630 IU
Calcium	48 mg
Magnesium	34 mg
Potassium	352 mg
Manganese	0.2 mg

Roasted butternut squash

SERVES 4 (G) (A)

1 butternut squash,
    about 450 g/1 lb
1 onion, chopped
2–3 garlic cloves, crushed
4 small tomatoes, chopped
85 g/3 oz chestnut mushrooms,
    chopped
85 g/3 oz canned butter beans,
    drained, rinsed and roughly
    chopped
1 courgette, about 115 g/4 oz,
    trimmed and grated
1 tbsp chopped fresh oregano,
    plus extra to garnish
2 tbsp tomato purée
300 ml/10 fl oz water
4 spring onions, trimmed and
    chopped
1 tbsp Worcestershire or hot
    pepper sauce, or to taste
pepper

Method

1 Preheat the oven to 190°C/375°F/Gas Mark 5. Prick the squash all over with a metal skewer then roast for 40 minutes, or until tender. Remove from the oven and leave until cool enough to handle.

2 Cut the squash in half, scoop out and discard the seeds then scoop out some of the flesh, making hollows in both halves. Chop the scooped out flesh and put in a bowl. Place the two halves side by side in a large roasting tin.

3 Add the onion, garlic, chopped tomatoes and mushrooms to the squash flesh in the bowl. Add the butter beans, courgette, oregano and a little pepper, to taste, and mix well. Spoon the filling into the 2 halves of the squash, packing it down as firmly as possible.

4 Mix the tomato purée with the water, spring onions and Worcestershire sauce in a small bowl and pour around the squash.

5 Cover loosely with a large sheet of foil and bake for 30 minutes, or until piping hot. Serve in warmed bowls, garnished with oregano.

79

BLUEBERRIES

The deep colour of blueberries indicates their high levels of proanthocyanidins. These support circulation, a crucial factor in late pregnancy.

With an extra 40–50 per cent of blood flowing around the body, it is imperative that the blood vessels stay intact and strong. Proanthocyanidins help with this, along with the vitamins C and A that are also present in blueberries. Easy bruising, varicose veins, nosebleeds and haemorrhoids are common symptoms that result from damage to blood vessels. Effective circulation also ensures good skin condition, brain function and a steady supply of oxygen and nutrients to the placenta and baby; any break in the flow can be detrimental. Proanthocyanidins are also believed to neutralize the enzymes that cause inflammation and can damage connective tissue, relieving pregnancy aches and pains, including discomfort in the joints, carpal tunnel and pelvic girdle pain.

- Provide proanthocyanidin circulatory support to help prevent haemorrhoids, varicose veins and easy bruising.
- Healthy blood flow ensures the baby receives a constant supply of oxygen and nutrients.
- A naturally anti-inflammatory food that helps relieve common pregnancy symptoms, including joint pains.

Practical tips:
Blueberries can be easily frozen and enjoyed whenever convenient, either as a snack or in smoothies or yogurt. They are a perfect food to graze on during labour because they are digested quickly and will help keep oxygen flowing to the contracting muscles.

DID YOU KNOW?

Blueberries and other strong antioxidant foods support the production of your immune antibodies. These are able to pass through the placenta and give protection directly to the baby.

MAJOR NUTRIENTS PER 100 G/3½ OZ BLUEBERRIES

Kcalories	57
Total fat	0.33 g
Protein	0.74 g
Carbohydrate	14.49 g
Fibre	2.4 g
Vitamin C	9.7 mg
Vitamin A	54 IU
Lutein/Zeaxanthin	80 mcg

Blueberry nectar

SERVES 1–2 (A)(V)(Q)

1 pear, peeled and cored
150 g/5½ oz blueberries
100 g/3½ oz natural bio yogurt
½ tsp honey
2 tsp flaked almonds

Method

1 Put the pear and blueberries into a food processor or blender. Add the yogurt and honey and blend until smooth and frothy. Pour into glasses, sprinkle with the almonds and serve.

5

Postnatal Nutrition

Postnatal nutrition is all about recovery, healing and helping you cope with the after-effects of birth. Bringing down inflammation and preventing infection around the birth area is an obvious priority, but pain relief, ease of bowel movements and milk flow can also be helped by dietary factors.

Quality, sustaining foods help support energy and mood, and provide you with vital anti-depressant nutrients like zinc, B vitamins and magnesium. If breastfeeding, this is doubly important because your recovery and health can suffer as you provide your baby with the nutrients it needs to thrive and grow. Milk production can require as much as 500 extra calories a day in energy, and that needs to come from nutrient-dense food.

(G) Growth of baby
(B) Brain development of baby
(A) Immunity-supporting antioxidants
(N) Natural remedy
(V) Suitable for vegetarians
(Q) Quick and easy to prepare

80

FENNEL

Fennel is rich in phytoestrogens, which means that it supports the hormones that maintain healthy milk supply. Foods that can do this are called galactogogues.

Foods that are high in phytoestrogens, such as soy, are not recommended after birth, but the levels in fennel provide gentle and balanced support without overloading the baby's delicate hormones. The antioxidants in fennel also help prevent infections, making this an excellent recovery food. The vitamin C content, along with the bioflavonoids rutin and quercetin work hard to keep the blood vessels intact, helping to calm post-birth bleeding, encourage wound healing, and prevent haemorrhoids. These nutrients are also anti-inflammatory so they help to relieve swelling and discomfort, while the vitamin C in combination with the sulphur in fennel produces collagen, promoting the healing of all the body's tissues. Fennel has been used traditionally to treat digestive complaints, such as gas and bloating, to help shed excess fluid and to regulate blood pressure, all of which may be problems after birth.

- A galactagogue food, traditionally used to bring on milk supply.
- Antioxidants vitamin C, quercetin and rutin help prevent infections, reduce inflammation and support healing.
- Vitamin C and sulphur help healing through collagen generation.
- Supports digestion, fluid and blood pressure regulation post-birth.

Practical tips:
Sliced raw fennel adds a pleasing, fresh aniseed taste to salads. It can also be braised and served as a side dish, added to soups or included in juices to boost their cleansing power.

DID YOU KNOW?

Fennel seeds have a long tradition of use in postnatal recovery. Mothers across the world drink fennel seed tea both to boost milk production and to relieve stomach complaints, whether in themselves or the baby.

MAJOR NUTRIENTS PER HALF BULB FENNEL

Kcalories	36.5
Total fat	0.24 g
Protein	1.45 g
Carbohydrate	8.53 g
Fibre	3.65 g
Vitamin C	14.1 mg
Folate	31.5 mcg
Potassium	484.5 mg

Salmon and fennel salad

SERVES 2 (A) (N) (Q)

300 g/10½ oz new potatoes, scrubbed

2 x 125 g/4½ oz skinless salmon fillets

55 g/2 oz butterhead lettuce leaves

25 g/1 oz baby spinach leaves

85 g/3 oz fennel, thinly sliced

1 cooked beetroot, diced

2 tbsp diced red onion

4-cm/1½-inch piece cucumber, seeded and diced

Dressing

6 tbsp sour cream

2 tbsp lemon juice

1 tbsp snipped fresh chives

4 sprigs dill, fronds chopped

1 tbsp extra virgin olive oil

1 tbsp water

pepper

Method

1 Cook the potatoes in boiling water for 10 minutes or until tender; drain and set aside.

2 Line the grill rack with foil and preheat the grill to high. Grill the salmon for 6–8 minutes, depending on the thickness of the fillets, turning once, until cooked.

3 Meanwhile, divide the lettuce and spinach between two plates. Top with the fennel, beetroot, onion and cucumber. Mix together the ingredients for the dressing.

4 Either top the salad with the whole salmon fillets or flake the fish and place on top. Drizzle the dressing over before serving.

81

WALNUTS

Walnuts supply some of the extra energy a mother needs to look after a new baby, while also encouraging healing and recovery after birth.

The mixture of beneficial oils, quality protein and complex carbohydrates in walnuts help to keep up energy, mood and milk supply at this time. The effectiveness is accentuated by the B-vitamin, zinc, magnesium and manganese content. Lots of protein is supplied to the baby in breast milk, so a mother's healing can suffer if her dietary intake is low. Walnuts are a natural mood food because they are instrumental in producing the 'happy' brain chemical serotonin. The hormone melatonin, present in walnuts, helps us fall asleep easily and sleep well when we do – when your sleep is being broken on a nightly basis, quality is essential.

- Contain balanced carbohydrates, protein and fats, to supply sustained energy for milk supply and a demanding schedule.
- The B vitamins, zinc, magnesium and manganese allow the best possible energy to be obtained from all the foods you eat.
- Protein and nutrients encourage serotonin production, helping to combat any postnatal depression.
- The hormone melatonin enables a new mother to snatch the best quality sleep when she can.

Practical tips:
Snack on raw, unsalted walnuts when breastfeeding or looking after the baby to promote good blood sugar balance and to avoid energy lows. This will also help to keep calorie intake regular, ensuring a consistent milk supply.

DID YOU KNOW?

Walnuts help keep up zinc levels, which are often low in nursing women. Zinc is directed as a priority to breast milk in order to support the baby's growth, but it is also vital for a mother's own healing.

MAJOR NUTRIENTS PER 25 G/1 oz WALNUTS

Kcalories	196
Total fat	19.5 g
Monounsaturated fat	2.68 g
Omega-3 fatty acids	2,728 mg
Omega-6 fatty acids	11,428 mg
Omega-9 fatty acids	2,639 mg
Protein	4.57 g
Carbohydrate	4.1 g
Fibre	2 g
Vitamin B3	0.34 mg
Vitamin B5	0.17 mg
Vitamin B6	0.16 mg
Magnesium	47.4 mg
Potassium	132 mg
Manganese	1.02 mg
Selenium	1.47 mcg
Zinc	0.93 mg
Phytosterols	32.4 mg

Bean and walnut salad

SERVES 2 Ⓖ Ⓐ Ⓥ Ⓠ

450 g/1 lb French beans
1 small onion, finely chopped
1 garlic clove, chopped
4 tbsp freshly grated
   Parmesan cheese
2 tbsp chopped walnuts, to garnish

Dressing

2 tbsp cider vinegar
6 tbsp olive oil
2 tsp chopped fresh tarragon

Method

1 Bring a large saucepan of water to the boil, add the beans and cook for 5 minutes, or until just tender. Remove with a slotted spoon and refresh the beans under cold running water. Drain and put into a mixing bowl and add the onion, garlic and cheese.

2 To make the dressing, put all the ingredients in a small screw-top jar and shake until well blended. Pour over the salad, cover with clingfilm and chill for at least 30 minutes.

3 Remove the salad from the refrigerator, give it a quick stir and transfer to serving dishes. Sprinkle the walnuts over the salad and serve.

82

BANANAS

Bananas provide good levels of potassium, the mineral needed for fluid balance and to enable the muscle contractions that shrink the uterus back to normal size.

A breastfed baby will take large amounts of its mother's potassium for its developing nervous system and muscles. A mother who is left deficient may suffer headaches, fatigue or muscle cramps. Bananas also deliver a healthy dose of vitamin C, which along with the tryptophan and vitamin B6, helps to lift mood, promote sleep and combat postnatal depression. These nutrients also encourage regular and easy bowel movements, at a time when haemorrhoids are common. As well as softening stools, the fibre inulin in bananas helps keep the body's beneficial probiotic bacteria at healthy levels. This is vital for immune health during recovery, and for keeping infection at bay.

- High potassium content supplies a mother's needs and is also required in breast milk for the baby's brain and muscle function.
- Vitamin C, B6 and tryptophan help produce serotonin for good mood and sleep.
- Support healthy bowel movements to help prevent haemorrhoids.
- Contain the fibre inulin, which promotes healthy gut bacteria for immune health and the prevention of infection.

Practical tips:
Bananas with raw nuts are the perfect snack because the added protein slows down the sugar release of the bananas. Bananas that are less ripe release their sugars into the bloodstream more slowly, supplying a more controlled form of energy.

DID YOU KNOW?

Bananas are used by athletes to maintain energy levels as they push their bodies to extremes. A new mother, facing similar demands, can boost her energy in the same way.

MAJOR NUTRIENTS PER MEDIUM-SIZED BANANA

Kcalories	105
Total fat	0.39 g
Protein	1.29 g
Fibre	3.1 g
Carbohydrate	26.95 g
Vitamin C	10.3 mg
Vitamin B6	0.43 mg
Potassium	422 mg
Tryptophan	11 mg

Indian rice pudding with banana

SERVES 2 ⓑ ⓐ ⓥ

100 g/3½ oz brown rice
350 ml/12 fl oz milk
3 cardamom pods, split
200 ml/7 fl oz water
1 tsp ground cinnamon, plus extra
   to serve
1 tsp vanilla bean paste or extract
1 heaped tbsp clear honey, plus
   extra to serve
finely grated zest of 1 small orange
1 large banana, sliced
1 tbsp flaked almonds

Method

1 Put the rice in a heavy-based saucepan with the milk, cardamom and the water. Bring to the boil, then reduce the heat to the lowest setting and simmer, covered, for 25–30 minutes, until the rice is tender (there should still be some liquid in the pan).

2 Remove from the heat, stir in the cinnamon, vanilla, honey and orange zest and leave to stand, covered, for 5 minutes.

3 Spoon the rice into serving bowls and top with the banana and almonds. Sprinkle with extra cinnamon and drizzle with honey before serving.

186 ✱ postnatal nutrition

83 SWEET POTATO

Sweet potatoes help strengthen immunity. Including them in the diet when breast-feeding results in more disease-attacking antibodies being passed to the baby.

Sweet potatoes provide calcium in balance with magnesium, enabling these two minerals to work at their most efficient in our bones and nervous system. We often receive these minerals in unbalanced amounts; dairy foods, for example, are high in calcium but relatively low in magnesium. While breastfeeding, the body's mineral levels need to be as high as during pregnancy, because the baby will take calcium in breast milk for use in bone development. If you have known problems with bone or tooth density, it is especially important to keep up your calcium levels. Even a non-breastfeeding mother may have lost calcium bone stores while pregnant. Sweet potatoes are also an excellent source of the antioxidant beta carotene, which will help rid the body of harmful toxins. The vitamin C content also helps provide collagen, which contributes to bone mass.

- Provides calcium in balance with magnesium for the most effective support to bone growth.
- Calcium is needed in breast milk for the baby's bone growth; if it doesn't come from the diet, it is taken from the mother's bones.
- Vitamin C helps generate collagen, which supports bone structure.

Practical tips:
Use in the same way as white potatoes or any root vegetable. Eat sweet potatoes with a little oil, such as olive oil or butter, because this will enable your body to absorb their fat-soluble nutrients.

DID YOU KNOW?
Calcium and magnesium are called the 'calming minerals' because they reduce anxiety and help us relax and fall asleep. They are especially important at a time when the body needs to conserve energy for recovery.

MAJOR NUTRIENTS PER 100 G/3.5 oz SWEET POTATO

Kcalories	86
Total fat	trace
Protein	1.6 g
Carbohydrate	20.1 g
Fibre	3 g
Vitamin C	2.4 mg
Vitamin E	0.27 mg
Calcium	30 mg
Magnesium	25.3 mg
Potassium	337.3 mg
Iron	0.6 mg
Selenium	0.6 mcg
Beta carotene	8,506.7 mcg

Baked sweet potatoes with ginger

SERVES 4   (G) (A) (V)

4 sweet potatoes, about
    300 g/10½ oz each
vegetable oil, for brushing
50 g/1¾ oz butter
40 g/1½ oz fresh ginger, sliced into
    very thin matchsticks
2 tbsp chopped fresh coriander
pepper

Method

1 Preheat the oven to 230°C/450°F/Gas Mark 8. Brush the
   sweet potatoes with oil and bake in the preheated oven for
   40–45 minutes, until tender. Cut a cross in the top of each potato.
   Press the flesh upwards until it bursts through the cuts.

2 Heat the butter in a frying pan over a medium–high heat, until
   foaming. Add the ginger and cook for 3–4 minutes, until golden
   and crisp.

3 Pour the ginger and buttery juices over the potatoes. Sprinkle with
   the coriander, season to taste with pepper, and serve.

84 APRICOTS

Apricots help maintain bowel regularity. Pectin, the fibre in apricots, helps soften stools and remove toxins that may enter breast milk from the body.

After childbirth, bowel movements are not always easy and the problem can be exacerbated by dehydration. It is particularly important to obtain plenty of water from vegetables and fruits, such as apricots, because their natural sugars will help to draw water into the body cells. The beta carotene content in apricots is converted to vitamin A by the body to heal and strengthen skin that has been torn, cut or stretched. It is also needed in breast milk for the baby's immune system and the development of his or her sight, taste and hearing. Vitamin A, along with the vitamin C content of apricots, is needed to utilize iron to take oxygen to tissues that require healing, and to replace any blood lost during childbirth.

- Help ease bowel movements, and therefore eliminate toxins, through good hydration and the fibre pectin.
- Vitamin A helps heal skin after pregnancy and childbirth.
- Vitamin A content in breast milk supports the baby's immunity and sensory abilities.
- Vitamins A and C enable iron to oxygenate the blood for healing and to replace any blood loss.

Practical tips:
Make into a purée by blending with boiling water. Keep in the fridge for a few days as a healthy sweetener for porridge, yogurt and cereal. Add cinnamon to enable the slow-release sugars to work even more effectively.

DID YOU KNOW?

Do not buy dried apricots containing the preservative sulphur dioxide. It can cause digestive discomfort, as well as headaches and asthma, and may pass into breast milk.

MAJOR NUTRIENTS PER 3 DRIED APRICOTS

Kcalories	47
Total fat	trace
Protein	1.2 g
Carbohydrate	10.8 g
Fibre	1.9 g
Vitamin C	trace
Potassium	414 mg
Iron	1 mg
Beta carotene	163 mcg

Apricot crumble

SERVES 6 Ⓖ Ⓐ Ⓝ Ⓥ

unsalted butter, for greasing
500 g/1 lb 2 oz fresh apricots,
    stoned and sliced
2 tbsp water
1 tsp ground cinnamon
Greek-style yogurt, to serve

Crumble topping

175 g/6 oz wholemeal flour
50 g/1¾ oz unsalted butter
50 g/1¾ oz brown sugar
50 g/1¾ oz hazelnuts, finely
    chopped

Method

1 Preheat the oven to 200°C/400°F/Gas Mark 6. Grease a 1.2-litre/
   2-pint ovenproof dish with a little unsalted butter.
2 To make the crumble topping, put the flour in a bowl and rub in
   the unsalted butter. Stir in the sugar and then the hazelnuts.
3 Arrange the apricots in the bottom of the prepared dish and add the
   water and cinnamon. Sprinkle the crumble topping evenly over
   the fruit until it is covered. Transfer to the preheated oven and bake
   for about 25 minutes until golden. Serve hot with Greek-style yogurt.

85 LENTILS

Hearty foods such as lentils help a new mother to lose her pregnancy weight safely. They provide constant energy at a time when restricting food is ill-advised.

MAJOR NUTRIENTS PER 100 G/3½ OZ DRIED LENTILS

Kcalories	353
Total fat	1.06 g
Protein	25.8 g
Carbohydrate	60.08 g
Fibre	30.5 g
Vitamin B1	0.87 mg
Vitamin B2	0.21 mg
Vitamin B3	2.61 mg
Vitamin B5	2.14 mg
Vitamin B6	0.54 mg
Folate	479 mcg
Magnesium	122 mg
Iron	7.54 mg
Manganese	1.33 mg
Selenium	8.3 mcg
Zinc	4.78 mg

When recovering from birth, and while breastfeeding, prioritising the high energy needs of these processes is more important than worrying about losing the weight gained during pregnancy. The B vitamins, zinc, fibre, complex carbohydrates and protein in lentils allow their energy to be released extremely efficiently, resulting in steady blood sugar balance. The zinc content of lentils also supports wound healing and immunity. If breastfeeding, the iron and folate (folic acid) will help to keep the baby's blood circulating. The magnesium and folate in lentils are also needed for brain and nerve function.

- Dense nutritional package that supports sustained energy for healing, recuperation and breast milk production.
- Consistent supply of slow-release energy prevents cravings for sugary foods with low nutrient content.
- Contain zinc for immune system support and healing.
- Contain iron and folate for the baby's blood.
- Contain magnesium and folate for the development of the baby's nervous system.

Practical tips:

A breastfeeding mother who tends to suffer from gas after eating lentils may find this affects the baby, too. Lentils can be more easily digested if soaked overnight. Throw away the soaking water with its problematic starches before cooking.

Vegetable and lentil casserole

SERVES 4   (G)(B)(A)(V)

3 cloves

1 onion, peeled but left whole

200 g/7 oz Puy or green lentils

1 bay leaf

1.5 litres/2¾ pints vegetable stock

2 leeks, sliced

2 potatoes, diced

2 carrots, chopped

3 courgettes, sliced

1 celery stalk, chopped

1 red pepper, deseeded and chopped

1 tbsp lemon juice

pepper

Method

1 Preheat the oven to 180°C/350°F/Gas Mark 4. Press the cloves into the onion. Put the lentils into a large casserole, then add the onion and bay leaf and pour in the stock. Cover and cook in the preheated oven for 1 hour.

2 Remove the onion and discard the cloves. Slice the onion and return it to the casserole with the vegetables. Stir thoroughly and season to taste with pepper. Cover and return to the oven for 1 hour.

3 Discard the bay leaf. Stir in the lemon juice and serve straight from the casserole.

86

ALFALFA

Sprouting seeds, such as alfalfa, contain all the nutrients needed for the most important growing phase in a young plant's life. Humans need these too.

The perfect amino acid (protein) content of alfalfa helps wounds heal, keeps toxins out of breast milk and helps prevent or clear up any infections that can occur after childbirth. Meanwhile, the antioxidants, vitamins A and C and beta carotene, support immune function and help the body to repair itself efficiently. In many traditional medicines, alfalfa is prescribed to improve the quality and flow of breast milk because of its action as a mild phytoestrogen food. It is also used for soothing digestive complaints because its enzymes can help break down food to relieve gas and constipation, which may add to postpartum haemorrhoids and pain. In addition, alfalfa is a rich source of the energizing and detoxifying plant pigment chlorophyll.

- Quality protein content promotes healing, healthy breast milk, and our ability to fight infection.
- Alkalizing and antioxidant-rich food that helps bring down inflammation, repair wounds and relieve pain.
- Traditional galactagogue, promoting healthy milk flow.
- Digestive aid that eases wind, constipation and haemorrhoids.

Practical tips:
Sprinkle on salads, or use in sandwiches and wraps to add a fresh taste and crunchy texture. It can be bought ready-sprouted in health food shops or grown at home in a sprouting jar. Eat raw to preserve the nutrients, but keep it cool as it wilts easily in heat.

DID YOU KNOW?

Alfalfa, and other plant foods, can provide a good amount of our daily water needs. Dehydration while breastfeeding can result in a poor uptake of water-soluble B vitamins and vitamin C in breast milk.

MAJOR NUTRIENTS PER 40 G/1½ OZ ALFALFA

Kcalories	9.2
Total fat	0.28 g
Protein	1.60 g
Carbohydrate	0.84 g
Fibre	0.76 g
Vitamin C	3.28 mg
Vitamin A	62 IU
Vitamin B3	0.19 mg
Vitamin B5	0.22 mg
Vitamin K	30.5 mcg
Choline	5.76 mg
Beta carotene	34.8 mcg
Calcium	12.8 mg
Magnesium	10.8 mg

Rice paper parcels with alfalfa

MAKES 8 Ⓖ Ⓐ Ⓝ Ⓥ Ⓠ

25 g/1 oz rice vermicelli noodles
8 dried rice paper wrappers
70 g/2½ oz cooked chicken breast,
    thinly sliced
2 spring onions, shredded
4-cm/1½ inch piece cucumber,
    quartered lengthways,
    deseeded and thinly sliced
handful alfalfa
3 tbsp chopped fresh basil
3 tbsp chopped fresh mint

Dipping sauce

2 tbsp fish sauce
1 tbsp light soy sauce
juice of ½ lime
½ tsp light brown sugar
½ tsp dried chilli flakes

Method

1 To make the dipping sauce, mix together all the ingredients in a small bowl.

2 Put the noodles in a bowl and cover with just-boiled water. Stir to separate the noodles, cover, and leave for about 4 minutes, until tender. Drain then refresh under cold running water; set aside.

3 Fill a large bowl with hot water. Carefully dunk a rice paper wrapper into the water and leave for a few seconds until soft and pliable. Lift out the wrapper and lay flat on a work surface; take care as they tear easily.

4 Arrange a heaped tablespoon of the noodles in a row in the centre of the wrapper, leaving space at the sides. Top with a few pieces of chicken, spring onion, cucumber, alfalfa, basil and mint, then fold in the sides of the wrapper and roll up to make a parcel. Continue, making 8 parcels in total. Serve with the dipping sauce.

87 FENUGREEK

Fenugreek is a useful food for women
who are having difficulty breastfeeding.
It has a long history in many cultures as a
galactagogue, or milk-promoting substance.

Fenugreek and various other foods, including alfalfa, dill, fennel and asparagus are all known galactagogues. Including some of them in the diet will encourage milk supply and quality when there are problems. Fenugreek is also good at balancing blood sugar levels, which means it levels out highs and lows of energy. It contains potent levels of several antioxidants, including apigenin, rutin and quercetin. Some studies have even shown that it boosts levels of other antioxidants in the body, helping to prevent damage to our body tissues. When included as part of a healthy diet, it will help provide energy to cells for healing and bring down inflammation, speeding the recovery process and relieving pain. Fenugreek may also help reduce excess mucus, so it may help to clear up any nasal congestion or digestive problems hanging around after pregnancy.

• Promotes good quality milk supply in breastfeeding mothers.
• Helps balance blood sugar levels for sustained energy.
• Antioxidant mix heals and soothes inflamed tissues.
• Helps reduce mucus to relieve nasal and digestive problems.

Practical tips:
To boost lactation, fenugreek is typically taken as a tea. Capsules or tinctures can be taken under the guidance of a qualified herbalist. Fenugreek may interact with some medications, and can also cause problems in women with asthma, allergies or diabetes, so please check with your healthcare provider first.

DID YOU KNOW?
Fenugreek contains a compound called trigonelline, a potent antioxidant known to help stimulate the regeneration of brain cells. This is what gives fenugreek (and coffee) its pungent bitter taste.

MAJOR NUTRIENTS PER 15 G/1 TBSP FENUGREEK SEEDS

Kcalories	36
Total fat	0.71 g
Protein	2.55 g
Carbohydrate	6.48 g
Fibre	2.7 g
Calcium	20 mg
Magnesium	21 mg
Potassium	85 mg
Phosphorus	33 mg
Iron	3.72 mg

Fenugreek tea

SERVES 2   Ⓐ Ⓝ Ⓥ Ⓠ

600 ml/1 pint water
2 tsp fenugreek seeds
1 tsp clear honey (optional)
ice cubes and lemon slices,
   to serve (optional)

Method

1 Pour the water into a saucepan and bring to the boil. Add the seeds and boil for 5 minutes.

2 Remove from the heat and leave to steep for 10–15 minutes.

3 Strain and pour into two cups, adding honey to taste, if using. The tea can also be served as a refreshing cold drink with ice cubes and a slice of lemon.

88

DILL

Dill is a galactagogue herb so it promotes both the volume and quality of breast milk, helping a new mother deliver vital nutrients to her baby.

Even if a baby is only breastfed for a short time, dill in the mother's diet can help provide it with vital vitamin A, which is known to be lower in exclusively bottle-fed babies. Vitamin A helps prevent infectious disease. Babies with low levels of this vitamin have been known to suffer from poor growth, eye problems and diarrhoea. Dill is also an antibacterial agent, helping prevent the spread of infection in the mother that can hinder recovery and may affect the baby. Including as many calcium- and magnesium-rich foods as possible in the diet is particularly important if bones and teeth suffered during pregnancy. The vitamins A, C and B3 are also needed to keep up the mother's own bone mass.

- A galactagogue, promoting a good flow of healthy breast milk.
- Vitamin A ensures good levels in breast milk for the baby's health.
- Antibacterial agent that helps keep down the proliferation of infectious bacteria.
- Rich in bone and teeth-strengthening vitamins and minerals for both mother and breastfed baby.

Practical tips:

Dill has a delicate anise flavour, and can be added to everyday foods such as eggs, cottage cheese, potato salad and smoked salmon. Mix it with butter to give an extra dimension to crackers and toast. Make dill tea from the seeds or leaves to help calm an upset stomach and encourage sleep.

DID YOU KNOW?

Dill is the main ingredient in traditional herbal gripe waters for colicky babies. In India, mothers use a tea made from a mix of ajwain (carom seeds), cumin, fennel and dill weed.

MAJOR NUTRIENTS PER 15 G/½ OZ DILL

Kcalories	12.9
Total fat	0.2 g
Protein	0.52 g
Carbohydrate	1.05 g
Fibre	0.3 g
Vitamin C	12.8 mg
Vitamin B3	0.24 mg
Vitamin A	1,158 IU
Folate	22 mcg
Calcium	31 mg
Magnesium	8 mg
Potassium	111 mg
Phosphorus	10 mg
Iron	0.99 mg

Dill and peppercorn vinegar

MAKES 250 ML/9 FL OZ (G)(A)(N)(V)(Q)

6 sprigs fresh dill
250 ml/0 fl oz cider vinegar
1 tsp whole black peppercorns

Method

1 Wash and dry the dill.

2 In a saucepan over a medium heat, bring the vinegar to the boil. Reduce the heat and simmer for 2 minutes. Add the dill and peppercorns, turn off the heat and leave for 15 minutes until cooled.

3 Pour into a clean jar, seal and keep in a dark place until ready to use or refrigerate.

89 RYE

Rye provides slow-release energy because of its high fibre content. Its B vitamins do the job of unlocking this energy. The effect is good for the body and the mind.

MAJOR NUTRIENTS PER 100 G/3½ oz DARK RYE FLOUR

Kcalories	325
Total fat	2.22 g
Omega-6 fatty acids	958 mg
Protein	15.91 g
Carbohydrate	68.63 g
Fibre	23.8 g
Vitamin B1	0.32 mg
Vitamin B2	0.25 mg
Vitamin B3	4.27 mg
Vitamin B5	1.46 mg
Vitamin B6	0.44 mg
Vitamin A	11 IU
Magnesium	160 mg
Iron	4.97 mg
Manganese	6.06 mg
Selenium	18 mcg
Zinc	5.04 mg
Lutein/Zeaxanthin	210 mcg

The zinc in rye works in combination with vitamin B6 and magnesium to enable the body to produce the mood-enhancing brain chemical serotonin. Zinc is responsible for growth, too, so a breastfeeding mother's levels can be easily depleted in service of her baby's rapid growth rate. Zinc also promotes healing. An inadequate amount of this mineral can reduce milk supply by lowering prolactin levels, the hormone responsible for signalling milk production. Zinc is also responsible for transporting vitamin A to breast milk. Most babies are born with low levels of this vitamin, so they need to take it from breast milk in the first six months of life. Children with low levels show poor resistance to infection, decreased appetite and tendencies to iron-deficiency anaemia.

- The B vitamins, zinc and slow-release energy help the brain combat postnatal depression.
- Zinc is a crucial component both for the baby's growth and the mother's own repair mechanisms.
- Low zinc can result in a reduced milk supply and less vitamin A in breast milk, which can affect the baby's immunity and iron levels.

Practical tips:
Rye creates a dense, less fluffy bread. This helps regulate appetite because it takes longer to chew, and chewing tells the body it has received food. This can help you manage sugar cravings that occur when energy is low.

Eggs and peppers on rye toast

SERVES 4   (G) (B) (A) (V) (Q)

2 tbsp olive oil

1 small red pepper, deseeded
   and chopped

1 small red onion, very finely
   chopped

pinch of paprika, plus extra
   to garnish (optional)

4 slices dark rye bread

8 large eggs

4 tbsp milk

25 g/1 oz butter

pepper

Method

1   Heat half the oil in a non-stick frying pan over a medium–high heat,
add the red pepper and onion and cook, stirring frequently, for
10 minutes, or until soft. Add the paprika, stir and set aside.

2   Preheat the grill to high. Toast one side of the bread slices. Brush
the other sides with the remaining oil, then lightly toast. Keep warm.

3   Beat the eggs with the milk and a little pepper to taste in a bowl.
Melt the butter in a non-stick saucepan, add the egg mixture and
cook over a medium–high heat, stirring frequently to make sure that
the eggs don't stick, for 5 minutes, or until thoroughly cooked.

4   Gently stir in the red pepper mixture, then spoon onto the rye
toasts. Sprinkle with a little extra paprika to garnish, if using, and
serve immediately.

90

PSYLLIUM HUSK POWDER

Normalizing bowel movements after childbirth is a priority, and psyllium husk powder is an effective, gentle and safe way to ensure this.

Psyllium husk powder is the ground outer shell of the psyllium seed. It is used as a stool-softening agent because the powder easily absorbs water to form a large mass in the bowel. Psyllium seeds contain 10–30 per cent of a substance called mucilage that becomes gelatinous on contact with water. This property regulates water in the bowel, bulking out stools so they can be more easily moved in cases of constipation, and drawing out water to firm-up stools in cases of diarrhoea. It also helps relieve the pain of passing a stool when this is likely to put pressure on sore areas or a wound.

- Safe stool-softening mucilage that regulates bowel movements post-birth.
- Regulates water in stools to reduce the incidence of both constipation and diarrhoea.

Practical tips:
Psyllium husk powder is available at most health food shops. If you are breastfeeding, buy the pure powder and not one mixed with senna. Sufficient water must be drunk over the course of the day to ensure the psyllium doesn't cause further blockages. Drink at least 225 ml (8 fl oz) of fluids for every 3–5 grams of husk taken. The usual dose is 1 teaspoon (approximately 5 grams) three times per day, but start with half that dose and build up, to avoid the possibility of an initial worsening of gas or bloating. Psyllium husk powder is most effective when taken with meals.

DID YOU KNOW?

The soluble fibre content of psyllium husk powder has been found to help regulate blood sugar in people with diabetes, which makes it a particularly useful preparation for diabetic new mothers. It is safe to take while breastfeeding.

MAJOR NUTRIENTS PER 5 G/1 TSP PSYLLIUM HUSK POWDER

Kcalories	7
Total fat	0 g
Protein	0 g
Carbohydrate	2 g
Fibre	1.8 g
Calcium	4.32 mg
Iron	0.03 mg

Apple, carrot and cucumber juice

SERVES 1   (A) (N) (V) (Q)

1 apple, unpeeled, cored
   and chopped
1 carrot, peeled and chopped
½ cucumber, chopped
225 ml/8 fl oz water
1 tsp psyllium husk powder
pieces of carrot, cucumber and
   apple on a cocktail stick,
   to decorate

Method

1 Place the apple, carrot, cucumber and water into a food processor
   or blender and process.
2 Pour into a glass and stir in the psyllium husk powder. Set the
   cocktail stick on top of the glass. Serve and drink immediately.

91

SPINACH

The dark green colour of spinach demonstrates its high levels of protective carotenoid antioxidants, including vitamin A, beta carotene, lutein and zeaxanthin.

The carotenoids that protect the plant as it photosynthesizes, or draws energy from sunlight, also protect the fatty areas of our bodies. After birth this means the healing of damaged skin and tissues, helping bring down inflammation and creating new tissues as the womb and abdominal skin return to normal. Breast milk contains carotenoids at higher levels in the first few days of production. The reason for this is not fully understood but is believed to help a newborn's transition from the womb to the harsher outside world. Lutein remains high for longest, possibly to protect the baby's vulnerable eyes from exposure to light. The folate (folic acid) in spinach also supports the growth of both mother's and breastfed baby's new tissues. The vitamin K enables bone growth and, as the baby cannot make this, he or she has to rely on its presence in milk.

- Antioxidant carotenoids help heal post-birth damage.
- Supplies carotenoids for breast milk, protecting a new baby against light exposure.
- Folate supports healing and repair.
- Vitamin K is passed to the baby for steady bone development.

Practical tips:
Eating plenty of green leafy vegetables is one of the foundations of health. Vitamin C and folate are easily damaged by cooking, so lightly steaming is a more nutritious solution than boiling the leaves.

DID YOU KNOW?

Spinach contains both iron and vitamin C. The vegetable non-haem form of iron is less easily utilized than the animal haem form, and needs vitamin C to help its absorption.

MAJOR NUTRIENTS PER 100 G/3½ OZ SPINACH

Kcalories	23
Total fat	0.4 g
Protein	2.2 g
Carbohydrate	3.6 g
Fibre	2.2 g
Vitamin C	28 mg
Vitamin A	9,377 IU
Beta carotene	5,626 mcg
Vitamin E	2.03 mg
Vitamin K	483 mcg
Folate	194 mcg
Calcium	99 mg
Magnesium	79 mg
Iron	2.71 mg
Lutein/Zeaxanthin	12,198 mcg

Mushroom, spinach and rice burgers

SERVES 4–6 (G) (A)

25 g/1 oz brown rice
4 tbsp olive oil
3–4 garlic cloves, crushed
300 g/10½ oz button mushrooms,
chopped
175 g/6 oz fresh spinach leaves
300 g/10½ oz canned borlotti
beans, drained
1 orange pepper, deseeded, peeled
and finely chopped
55 g/2 oz flaked almonds
55 g/2 oz Parmesan cheese,
grated
2 tbsp chopped fresh basil
55 g/2 oz fresh wholemeal
breadcrumbs
2 tbsp wholemeal flour
1–2 beef tomatoes, thickly sliced
4–6 large field mushrooms
pepper

Method

1 Cook the rice in a saucepan of boiling water for 20–25 minutes, or until tender. Drain and place in a food processor.

2 Heat 1 tablespoon of the oil in a frying pan. Add the garlic and button mushrooms and cook for 5 minutes. Add to the rice in the food processor.

3 Reserve 25 g/1 oz spinach leaves. Add the remaining spinach, the beans, pepper, almonds, Parmesan cheese, basil, breadcrumbs and pepper to taste to the rice

mixture in the food processor and, using the pulse button, chop finely. Mix well, then shape into 4–6 equal-sized burgers. Coat in the flour, then cover and leave to chill in the refrigerator for 1 hour.

4 Preheat the grill to medium–high. Heat 2 tablespoons of the oil in a non-stick frying pan and cook the burgers for 5–6 minutes each side, or until golden and cooked through. Meanwhile, brush the tomato slices and mushrooms with the remaining oil and grill for 6–8 minutes, turning once, until softened.

5 Place the reserved spinach leaves on individual serving plates and top each with a mushroom. Add the burgers and tomato slices and serve immediately.

92 PLUMS

Along with berries and apples, plums rank in the top twenty foods in the ORAC table. These superfoods have the very best postnatal immune and healing potential.

The ORAC (Oxygen Radical Absorption Capacity) scale measures the antioxidant capacity of plants and identifies the foods we need to consume regularly in order to neutralize free radicals and help prevent diseases. After birth, when the body cannot afford to waste its energy on dealing with infections, these needs are at their highest. Eating plums, and other chart-topping ORAC foods, will help reduce the impact of milk production and the body's necessary healing work. Supporting your immune function in this way will also make the need for antibiotics less likely, which, if you're breastfeeding, can lead to oral thrush for your baby. Plums contain high levels of the potent antioxidant chlorogenic acid and also the soluble fibre pectin, which helps to keep the bowels healthy and toxins removed from the digestive tract.

- High antioxidant profile helps prevent inflammation and infection, allowing the body to use its energy for healing and producing milk.
- Help lower the likelihood of antibiotic use by supporting immunity.
- The fibre pectin eases bowel movements and prevents the absorption of toxins.

Practical tips:
Like apples and rhubarb, plums can be stewed to make a naturally gentle laxative. The result is delicious added to Bircher muesli, porridge or yogurt and will keep things moving without discomfort.

DID YOU KNOW?

Plums are naturally high in the chemical serotonin, which raises mood and can help ward off postnatal depression. Other happy foods are avocados, bananas, aubergine, pineapple, tomatoes and walnuts.

MAJOR NUTRIENTS PER AVERAGE-SIZED PLUM

Kcalories	30
Total fat	trace
Protein	0.5 g
Carbohydrate	7.5 g
Fibre	0.9 g
Vitamin C	6.3 mg
Vitamin K	4.2 mcg
Potassium	104 mg
Beta carotene	125 mcg
Lutein/Zeaxanthin	48 mcg

Spiced plum cupcakes

SERVES 4 (A) (V)

55 g/2 oz butter, softened, plus
   extra for greasing
55 g/2 oz caster sugar
1 large egg, lightly beaten
55 g/2 oz plain wholemeal flour
½ tsp baking powder
1 tsp ground mixed spice
25 g/1 oz blanched hazelnuts,
   coarsely ground
2 small plums, halved, stoned
   and sliced
Greek-style yogurt, to serve

Method

1 Preheat the oven to 180°C/350°F/Gas Mark 4. Grease 4 x
  150-ml/5-fl oz ovenproof teacups.

2 Put the butter and sugar in a bowl and beat together until light and
  fluffy. Gradually beat in the egg. Sift in the flour, baking powder and
  mixed spice (tipping any bran left in the sieve into the bowl) and,
  using a metal spoon, fold into the mixture with the ground hazelnuts.
  Spoon the mixture into the prepared teacups. Arrange the sliced
  plums on top of the mixture.

3 Put the teacups on a baking tray and bake in the preheated oven for
  25 minutes, or until risen and firm to the touch. Serve warm or cold
  with Greek-style yogurt.

93 SARDINES

Obtaining complete quality protein from sardines and other oily fish helps recovery and mood. The omega-3 fatty acids they contain are a vital component of breast milk.

DID YOU KNOW?

Sardines and other small oily fish, such as salmon, trout and mackerel, contain only low levels of mercury and can be eaten in moderation when breastfeeding. Avoid larger, contaminated fish such as tuna and swordfish.

MAJOR NUTRIENTS PER 135 G/5 OZ (ABOUT 3) SARDINES

Kcalories	280
Total fat	16 g
Omega-3 fatty acids – EPA	1,147 mg
Omega-3 fatty acids – DHA	1,550 mg
Protein	33 g
Carbohydrate	0 g
Fibre	0 g
Vitamin B3	7 mg
Vitamin B5	0.87 mg
Vitamin B12	15 mcg
Vitamin A	302.4 IU
Vitamin D	367.2 IU
Vitamin E	2.7 mg
Magnesium	53 mg
Potassium	536 mg
Iron	3.9 mg
Zinc	1.8 mg
Selenium	71 mcg

Studies clearly show that a mother's levels of dietary omega-3 fatty acids are reflected in her breast milk. This finding refers specifically to DHA, the direct form of omega-3 found only in oily fish and incorporated into our brain cells. Many studies have linked low DHA to an increased risk of Sudden Infant Death Syndrome (SIDS), the development of Attention Deficit Hyperactivity Disorder (ADHD), schizophrenia, poor sleep patterns, asthma, eczema, and lower IQ. Low levels in mothers are associated with postnatal depression. Sardines provide the vital brain and mood-supporting combination of quality protein, B vitamins, vitamins A and D and minerals.

- Direct form of DHA, resulting in healthy breast milk and a lowered risk of ADHD, asthma, eczema, poor brain development and mental health issues for the child.
- DHA in combination with protein, vitamins and minerals may help prevent postnatal depression, or milder unhappy feelings and weepiness.

Practical tips:

Due to possible contamination, the recommendation while breastfeeding is to eat 2 portions of oily fish a week. However, some scientists believe that the negative effects of too little DHA far outweigh the risk from toxins. You may prefer to take a fish oil supplement, but check with your healthcare provider first. Vegetarians should use a vegan marine algae source.

Sardines with Mediterranean spinach

SERVES 4   (G) (B) (A) (Q)

3 tbsp olive oil

finely grated rind and juice
    of 1 orange

1 small red onion, thinly sliced

1 garlic clove, very finely chopped

12 sprigs fresh thyme

12 sardines, heads removed,
    gutted and rinsed inside and out

chopped fresh coriander, to garnish

Mediterranean spinach

1½ tbsp olive oil

1 onion, chopped

1 large garlic clove, crushed

2 tsp ground coriander

2 tsp ground cumin

900 g/2 lb baby leaf spinach, rinsed

55 g/2 oz pine kernels, lightly
    toasted

pepper

Method

1 Put the olive oil, orange rind and juice, onion and garlic in a flat bowl large enough to hold all the sardines and whisk until blended. Put a thyme sprig inside each sardine, then add the fish to the marinade and use your hands to coat them.

2 To make the Mediterranean spinach, heat the oil in a frying pan over a medium–high heat. Add the onion and cook, stirring, for 3 minutes, then add the garlic and continue to cook, stirring, until the onion is soft. Stir in the coriander and cumin and continue to cook, stirring, for a minute.

3 Add the spinach with just the water clinging to its leaves, using a wooden spoon to push it into the pan, and add pepper to taste. Cook, stirring, for 6–8 minutes, or until the leaves are wilted. Sprinkle with the pine kernels, then cover and keep warm while you grill the sardines.

4 Preheat the grill to high. Line the grill pan with foil. Arrange the sardines in the pan, brush with the marinade and place 10 cm/4 inches beneath the heat. Grill for 1½ minutes.

5 Turn the fish then brush with more marinade and grill for 1½–2 minutes, until the fish is cooked through and the flesh flakes easily. Serve with the Mediterranean spinach.

94

ORANGES

Oranges are known to be high in healing and protective vitamin C, but they also provide an easily digested form of calcium that gives protection to postnatal bones.

MAJOR NUTRIENTS PER MEDIUM-SIZED ORANGE

Kcalories	65
Total fat	trace
Protein	1 g
Carbohydrate	16 g
Fibre	3.4 g
Vitamin C	64 mg
Vitamin A	298 IU
Folate	39.8 mcg
Calcium	61 mg
Potassium	238 mg
Lutein/Zeaxanthin	182 mcg

Calcium is of optimum importance during this time. Firstly, the stocks that were used during pregnancy for the development of the baby's skeleton need to be replaced. The chances are that some of that calcium was taken from the bones and teeth and not only from the diet. The needs of breastfeeding mothers must be kept up as they are continuing to provide calcium, vitamin C, vitamin A and folate (folic acid) for the baby's bones. Oranges contain vitamin C, needed to produce collagen, which is present in all of our body structures. Vitamin C cannot be stored in the body and should be consumed on a daily basis. Post-pregnancy, a lack can reveal itself in poor hair, nail and skin quality, and bones and teeth suffer. The antioxidants in oranges help to reduce inflammatory symptoms such as mastitis and poor wound healing.

- Calcium is supplied to the baby in breast milk, and ensures the mother's bone and teeth stay at optimum health after pregnancy.
- Vitamin C promotes collagen for the repair of hair, skin and nails.
- High antioxidant load helps reduce inflammation that can lead to mastitis and poor healing capacity.

Practical tips:
Whole oranges are the best way to receive the nutrients. You get more of an antioxidant and healing boost from eating a fresh orange than drinking juice, and retaining the fibre means you avoid the risk of a sugar rush.

Exotic fruit cocktail

SERVES 4   Ⓖ Ⓐ Ⓥ Ⓠ

2 oranges
2 large passion fruit
1 pineapple
1 pomegranate
1 banana

Method

1 Cut 1 orange in half and squeeze the juice into a bowl, discarding any pips. Using a sharp knife, cut away all the peel and pith from the second orange. Working over the bowl to catch the juice, carefully cut the orange segments between the membranes to obtain skinless segments of fruit. Discard any pips.

2 Cut the passion fruit in half, scoop the flesh into a nylon sieve and, using a spoon, push the pulp and juice into the bowl of orange segments. Discard the pips.

3 Using a sharp knife, cut away all the skin from the pineapple and cut the flesh lengthways into quarters. Cut away the central hard core. Cut the flesh into chunks and add to the orange and passion fruit mixture. Cover and refrigerate the fruit at this stage if you are not serving immediately.

4 Cut the pomegranate into quarters and, using your fingers or a teaspoon, remove the red seeds from the membrane. Cover and refrigerate until ready to serve.

5 Just before serving, peel and slice the banana, add to the fruit cocktail with the pomegranate seeds and mix thoroughly. Serve immediately.

95

ROMAINE LETTUCE

The more anti-inflammatory foods that you eat, such as romaine lettuce, the greater your body's ability to soothe and heal inflamed body tissues.

Romaine lettuce contains plenty of vital folate (folic acid). This B vitamin plays a crucial role in all the body's growth and repair because it is needed to manufacture RNA and DNA proteins, our genetic materials. These tell the body how and when to provide new proteins for growth. Folate also helps the body make new red blood cells and immune system cells, for the breastfed baby, too. The bitter taste of the leaves helps stimulate bile flow, and therefore digestion, so that the body gets the most nutrients from the food you eat. The digestive system may still be slower immediately after birth, but this stimulation will reduce any tendencies to gas or constipation. The generous fibre levels in romaine also help to form easy-to-pass stools that won't aggravate a sore perineum.

- Folate enables growth and repair, and also produces red blood cells and immune cells for mother and breastfed baby.
- Sluggish digestion post-pregnancy is stimulated by the bitter taste.
- Fibre helps to soften stools, making them less painful to pass after childbirth.

Practical tips:
Romaine, or cos, lettuce can be eaten like any salad leaf. If constipated or suffering from gas, eat it regularly for its water content. The larger, sturdier leaves make a good alternative to wraps if you find bread or wheat products difficult to digest.

DID YOU KNOW?

People who eat fewer than three vegetables a day, or who rarely eat green leafy vegetables such as romaine lettuce, have been found to have inadequate levels of folate. The need for folate remains high post-pregnancy for healing and breast milk supply for your baby.

MAJOR NUTRIENTS PER 100 G/3½ OZ ROMAINE LETTUCE

Kcalories	17
Total fat	0.3 g
Protein	1.2 g
Carbohydrate	3.3 g
Fibre	2.1 g
Vitamin C	24 mg
Folate	136 mcg
Calcium	33 mg
Potassium	247 mg

Lettuce, chickpea and tomato salad

SERVES 4   (G) (A) (V) (Q)

400 g/14 oz canned chickpeas,
    drained and rinsed
225 g/8 oz ripe tomatoes, roughly
    chopped
1 small red onion, thinly sliced
handful fresh basil leaves, torn
1 romaine or cos lettuce, torn
fresh crusty bread, to serve

Dressing

1 clove garlic, crushed
juice and zest of 1 lemon
3 tbsp olive oil
1 tbsp water
pepper

Method

1 To make the dressing, put all the ingredients into a small screw-top jar and shake until well blended. Taste and add more lemon juice or oil, if necessary.

2 Put the chickpeas, tomatoes, onion and basil in a serving bowl and mix gently. Pour over the dressing and mix again. Arrange on a bed of lettuce and serve with crusty bread.

96 WATERMELON

Watermelon is high in the carotenoid lycopene, which gives it its red colour. This protective nutrient is passed to the baby in breast milk.

Eating a rainbow of fruits and vegetables ensures that the full spectrum of antioxidants is made available to both mother and breastfed baby, lowering the risk of infectious disease and inflammatory conditions, such as asthma, eczema and mastitis. The lycopene in watermelon specifically protects fatty areas of the body, including the brain, heart and liver. L-citrulline, an amino acid in the fruit, is converted by the body to L-arginine and helps reduce high blood pressure. This action is heightened by the potassium content of watermelon, which encourages levels to normalize in the stressful period post-pregnancy. The potassium and slow-release natural sugars help take watermelon's high water content into our cells for hydration. This is a crucial health concern post-pregnancy because so much fluid is lost in birth, and especially so while breastfeeding, when the body has to produce at least an extra pint of fluid a day.

- Antioxidant carotenoid provides protection to fatty areas of the brain, heart and liver post-birth; a breastfed baby also benefits.
- L-citrulline and potassium help normalize high blood pressure.
- High water content, potassium and natural sugars help hydration.

Practical tips:
Cut or juice watermelon immediately before eating to retain its vitamin C content. The antioxidant carotenoids are better absorbed with some oil present – add to a salad with an olive oil dressing, or enjoy after a meal.

DID YOU KNOW?

Vitamin C and lycopene help protect the heart from future disease risk – an important consideration when women's heart disease is on the rise, and pregnancy forces the heart to work 25 per cent harder.

MAJOR NUTRIENTS PER 100 G/3½ OZ WATERMELON

Kcalories	30
Total fat	0.15 g
Protein	0.61 g
Carbohydrate	7.55 g
Fibre	0.4 g
Vitamin C	8.1 mg
Potassium	112 mg
Lycopene	4,532 mcg
Beta carotene	303 mcg

Fruit cocktail with granola

SERVES 4 Ⓐ Ⓥ Ⓠ

25 g/1 oz rolled oats
1 tbsp sesame seeds
pinch of ground ginger
1 tbsp sunflower seeds
2 tsp freshly squeezed orange juice
1 tsp clear honey

Fruit cocktail

300 g/10½ oz watermelon, skin
*   removed, deseeded and*
*   cut into chunks*
100 g/3½ oz fresh orange
*   segments*
6 tbsp freshly squeezed
*   orange juice*
1 tsp finely grated orange zest
1 tsp peeled and finely sliced
*   ginger*
1 tsp clear honey

Method

1 Preheat the oven to 180°C/350°F/Gas Mark 4.
2 To make the granola, put all the dry ingredients into a bowl, then add the orange juice and honey and mix thoroughly. Spread out on a non-stick baking tray and bake for 7–8 minutes. Remove from the oven, break up into pieces, then return to the oven for a further 7–8 minutes. Remove from the oven and break up again. Leave to cool on the baking tray. The mixture will become crunchy when cool.
3 To make the fruit cocktail, put the watermelon and orange segments into a bowl. Put the orange juice and zest, ginger and honey into a small saucepan over a medium heat and bring to the boil. Pour the mixture over the fruit and leave to cool. Cover and chill in the refrigerator.
4 Spoon the fruit into bowls and sprinkle over the granola.

97 CRANBERRIES

After pregnancy, the kidneys and bladder can be susceptible to infection. Cranberries can help prevent these conditions, or soothe them if they have taken hold.

During the six weeks after birth, the kidneys have to work especially hard to help the body lose all the excess fluid it has been holding on to. The bladder is also recovering from being squashed by an expanded womb. These states can increase the risk of infections, including cystitis, which affects around 12 per cent of women after childbirth. Cranberries contain hippuric acid and antioxidant proanthocyanidins which have been shown to help prevent Urinary Tract Infections (UTIs), although they will not necessarily cure them once established. Anyone who is prone to cystitis should drink a preventative glass of cranberry juice a day to ward off infection. Cranberries rank as one of the top foods on the ORAC (Oxygen Radical Absorption Capacity) antioxidant index. For this reason, they can help to heal bladder and urinary tract tissues that may have been damaged during pregnancy and birth.

- Help prevent cystitis and bladder infections in women who are susceptible or had a catheter fitted after childbirth.
- High antioxidant capacity promotes the healing of tissues that are inflamed or damaged after pregnancy and labour.

Practical tips:
Cranberries are bitter so the juice drink is usually sweetened with sugar. For a healthier alternative, buy unsweetened cranberry juice from health food shops and mix with apple juice. One or two glasses a day should have the desired preventative effect.

DID YOU KNOW?
Research suggests that eating cranberries increases our levels of the beneficial gut bacteria *bifidobacterium*. This supports our natural immunity, and the protection is passed to a breastfed baby.

MAJOR NUTRIENTS PER 175 ML/6 FL OZ SWEETENED CRANBERRY JUICE

Kcalories	108
Total fat	trace
Protein	trace
Carbohydrate	26 g
Fibre	trace
Vitamin C	60 mg
Vitamin E	trace
Lutein/Zeaxanthin	150 mcg

MAJOR NUTRIENTS PER 100 G/3½ OZ CRANBERRIES

Kcalories	46
Total fat	trace
Protein	0.4 g
Carbohydrate	12.2 g
Fibre	4.6 g
Vitamin C	13 mg
Vitamin E	1.2 mcg
Lutein/Zeaxanthin	91 mcg

Chicken and cranberry salad

SERVES 4   (G) (B) (A) (N)

115 g/4 oz dried cranberries

2 tbsp fresh apple juice or water

200 g/7 oz sugar snap peas

2 ripe avocados, halved, stoned,
   peeled and sliced

juice of ½ lemon

4 lettuce hearts

1 bunch of watercress, trimmed

55 g/2 oz rocket

400 g/14 oz cooked chicken, sliced

55 g/2 oz chopped walnuts,
   to garnish (optional)

Dressing

2 tbsp olive oil

1 tbsp walnut oil

2 tbsp lemon juice

1 tbsp chopped fresh mixed herbs,
   such as parsley and
   lemon thyme

pepper

Method

1   Put the cranberries in a bowl. Stir in the apple juice, cover with
    clingfilm and leave to soak for 30 minutes. Meanwhile, blanch the
    sugar snap peas, refresh under cold running water and drain.

2   Toss the avocados in the lemon juice to prevent discoloration.
    Separate the lettuce hearts and arrange on a large serving platter with
    the avocados, sugar snap peas, watercress, rocket and chicken.

3   To make the dressing, put the first four ingredients into a small
    screw-top jar, with a little pepper to taste, and shake until combined.

4   Drain the cranberries and mix them with the dressing, then pour
    over the salad. Serve immediately, scattered with walnuts, if using.

98 BROAD BEANS

Broad beans contain L-dopa, from which we make the mood and motivation brain chemical dopamine, and so may help reduce the baby blues common after birth.

Broad beans are high in protein, magnesium, zinc and B vitamins, also important for production of dopamine and another mood-regulating neurotransmitter (brain chemical), serotonin. These qualities and the fibre and slow-release carbohydrates that help stop highs and lows of energy and mood are another factor to help reduce the likelihood of post-natal depression. High magnesium levels help to soothe the nervous system and ward off anxiety in your new situation, also helping you sleep when you get the chance. B vitamins, folate (folic acid), choline and zinc help the mechanisms that promote healing after childbirth.

- Help your body produce the mood neurotransmitters dopamine and serotonin to reduce the likelihood of post-natal depression.
- Slow-release food for sustained mood and energy levels.
- Magnesium helps keep you calm and able to sleep.
- B vitamins, folate, choline and zinc all work to promote optimal healing after labour.

Practical tips:
Broad beans must be cooked to break down alkaloids that can be harmful. They are prevalent in Greek and Mediterranean cuisine and can be used as well as chickpeas in falafel. They are Egypt's national food, made into *ful medames*, a type of dip. Broad beans are incredibly versatile, and can be used as any bean, added to soups, stews, salads and dips.

DID YOU KNOW?

Legumes like broad beans offer a good alternative to starchy carbohydrates such as bread, pasta and potatoes when you require lots of energy post-birth. They contain more protein and a variety of nutrients for your recovery phase.

MAJOR NUTRIENTS PER 100 G/3½ oz BROAD BEANS, UNCOOKED

Kcalories	341
Total fat	1.53 g
Protein	26.12 g
Carbohydrate	58.29 g
Vitamin B3	1.54 mg
Vitamin B5	1.59 mg
Folate	557 mcg
Choline	95.2 mg
Calcium	103 mg
Magnesium	192 mg
Potassium	1,062 mg
Iron	6.7 mg
Selenium	8.2 mcg

Spring stew

SERVES 4 (A) (Q)

2 tbsp olive oil

4–8 baby onions, halved

2 celery sticks, cut into
   5-mm/¼-inch slices

225 g/8 oz baby carrots,
   scrubbed and halved if large

300 g/10½ oz new potatoes,
   scrubbed and halved,
   or quartered if large

850 ml–1.2 litres/1½–2 pints
   vegetable stock

400 g/14 oz canned haricot beans,
   drained and rinsed

1 fresh bouquet garni

85 g/3 oz baby sweetcorn

115 g/4 oz frozen or shelled fresh
   broad beans, thawed if frozen

½–1 Savoy or spring (Primo)
   cabbage, about 225 g/8 oz

1½ tbsp cornflour

2 tbsp cold water

salt and pepper

55–85 g/2–3 oz Parmesan or
   mature Cheddar cheese, grated,
   to serve

Method

1 Heat the oil in a large, heavy-based saucepan, with a tight-fitting lid, and cook the vegetables, stirring frequently, for 5 minutes, or until softened.

2 Add the stock, beans and bouquet garni, then bring to the boil. Reduce the heat, cover and simmer for 12 minutes.

3 Add the baby sweetcorn and broad beans and season to taste with salt and pepper. Simmer for a further 3 minutes. Meanwhile, discard the outer leaves and hard central core from the cabbage and shred the leaves. Add to the saucepan and simmer for a further 3–5 minutes, or until all the vegetables are tender.

4 Blend the cornflour with the water, stir into the saucepan and cook, stirring, for 4–6 minutes, or until the liquid has thickened. Serve the cheese separately, for stirring into the stew.

99

SAVOY CABBAGE

Cabbage and other brassicas are an important immune-supporting part of any diet, but especially when the body's resources are low after childbirth.

Brassica vegetables contain detoxifying glucosinolate chemicals that help the body regulate hormonal changes after birth. Cabbage also contains significant levels of the amino acid glutamine, which keeps the gut healthy, supports muscle strength to help the body repair and cope, and has detoxifying and anti-inflammatory actions. Cabbage and other green leaves provide vitamin C and folate (folic acid), which we need to replenish daily as it is not easily stored in the body and is crucial for growth, wound repair, muscle building, energy production and brain and heart health. A mother who is breastfeeding needs to be particularly vigilant about her intake of these nutrients because she is also providing them to her baby. A daily intake is necessary to avoid deficiency symptoms.

- Glucosinolates aid hormonal balance and immune support.
- The amino acid glutamine promotes repair, supports muscle strength, reduces soreness and boosts digestive health.
- Provides essential vitamin C and folate for all growth and repair.

Practical tips:

Cabbage has been thought to cause gas in breastfed babies, but gas from the mother's intestines does not pass into breast milk, so any problems in the baby are more likely caused by an immature digestive system and swallowing air. Savoy cabbage relieves sore and engorged breasts in the early stages of breastfeeding; put a refrigerated leaf in each bra cup for simple and effective relief.

DID YOU KNOW?

Breastfed babies develop a taste for the foods their mothers eat, because the flavours pass into breast milk. A child is more likely to eat her greens if her mother did while breastfeeding.

MAJOR NUTRIENTS PER 100 G/3½ oz SAVOY CABBAGE

Kcalories	27
Total fat	trace
Protein	2 g
Carbohydrate	6.1 g
Fibre	3.1 g
Vitamin C	31 mg
Vitamin A	1,000 IU
Vitamin K	68.8 mcg
Folate	80 mcg
Calcium	35 mg
Magnesium	28 mg
Potassium	230 mg
Iron	0.7 mg
Manganese	0.2 mg
Selenium	0.9 mcg
Beta carotene	600 mcg